The Rational Guide To

Building Technical User Communities

PUBLISHED BY

Rational Press - An imprint of the Mann Publishing Group
208 Post Road, 2nd Floor
PO Box 519
Greenland, NH 03840, USA
www.rationalpress.com
www.mannpublishing.com
+1 (603) 601-0325

ISBN-10: 1-932577-32-7
ISBN-13: 978-1-932577-32-7
Library of Congress Control Number (LCCN): 2007929396
Printed and bound in the United States of America.
10 9 8 7 6 5 4 3 2

Trademarks

Mann Publishing, Mann Publishing Group, Agility Press, Rational Press, Inc.Press, NetImpress, Farmhouse Press, BookMann Press, The Rational Guide To, Rational Guides, ExecuGuide, AdminExpert, From the Source, the Mann Publishing Group logo, the Agility Press logo, the Rational Press logo, the Inc.Press logo, Timely Business Books, Rational Guides for a Fast-Paced World, and Custom Corporate Publications are all trademarks or registered trademarks of Mann Publishing Incorporated.

All brand names, product names, and technologies presented in this book are trademarks or registered trademarks of their respective holders.

Disclaimer of Warranty

While the publisher and author(s) have taken care to ensure accuracy of the contents of this book, they make no representation or warranties with respect to the accuracy or completeness of the contents of this book and specifically disclaim any implied warranties or merchantability or fitness for a specific purpose. The advice, strategies, or steps contained herein may not be suitable for your situation. You should consult with a professional where appropriate before utilizing the advice, strategies, or steps contained herein. Neither the publisher nor author(s) shall be liable for any loss of profit or any other commercial damages, including but not limited to special, incidental, consequential, or other damages.

Credits

Author:	Greg Low
Technical Editor:	Chris Wallace
Editorial Director:	Jeff Edman
Production Editor:	Kim Turner
Artist:	Scott Gardenhire
Indexer:	Christine Frank
Series Concept:	Anthony T. Mann
Cover Concept:	Marcelo Paiva
Special Thanks:	Stephen Price

All Mann Publishing Group books may be purchased at bulk discounts.

The Rational Guide To

Building Technical User Communities

Dr. Greg Low
Microsoft Regional Director

RATIONAL PRESS

An imprint of the **mann**
PUBLISHING GROUP

www.mannpublishing.com

Rational Guides for a
Fast-Paced World™

About Rational Guides

Rational Guides, from Rational Press, provide a no-nonsense approach to publishing based on both a practicality and price that make them rational. Each Rational Guide is constructed with the highest quality writing and production materials—at an affordable price. All Rational Guides are intended to be as complete as possible in a compact size. Furthermore, all Rational Guides come with bonus materials, such as additional chapters, applications, code, utilities, or other resources. To download these materials, just register your book at www.rationalpress.com. See the instruction page at the end of this book to find out how to register your book.

What's in this Book?

In this book, Greg has shared the most important lessons he has learned over decades of involvement in technical communities. It provides practical advice on establishing and (more importantly) sustaining and growing these communities. It helps the reader avoid common pitfalls and assists with important concepts such as growing your own speakers and provides tips for creating and delivering great presentations.

Who Should Read This Book

This book is designed for anyone with an interest in the dynamics of technical communities. It provides solid advice for those looking to create a new technical community and sage advice for those already organizing them. It also can assist those who are currently members of these communities to get the most out of their membership. The advice that is shared has been gleaned from long-term involvement in technical communities.

About the Author

Greg is a Senior Consultant for Readify Pty Ltd (www.readify.net) in Australia and heads up their SQL Server practice. He lives in Melbourne with his wife Mai. Greg has a passion for building technical communities. For over a decade, he organized the Queensland MSDN User Group and the Queensland SQL Server User Group and for many years was the chair of the user group relations committee for INETA in Asia Pacific. He holds a PhD in Computer Science from the Queensland University of Technology.

Greg co-founded CodeCampOz (www.codecampoz.com) with fellow Readifarian (and Microsoft MVP) Mitch Denny (www.notgartner.com) and is the founder of SQL Down Under, which operates an annual SQL Down Under Code Camp and a very popular podcast series (www.sqldownunder.com). He is a regular presenter at Microsoft and PASS events, user groups, code camps, and webcasts throughout the world. Microsoft has recognized Greg as a Microsoft MVP for SQL Server and in recent years as one of three Microsoft Regional Directors for Australia.

Dedication

No book, not even a relatively brief one, is the product of an individual. I must first thank Anthony Mann for his foresight and support regarding this uncommon book topic. I need to mention a number of people who have helped me in one way or another during my technical community journey. In no particular order and not a totally inclusive list, this would include: Charles (Chuck) Sterling, Andrew Coates, Mitch Denny, Dave Apelt, Mike Fitzsimon, James Whittred, Dave Glover, Frank Arrigo, Adam Cogan, Sanjay Shetty, Nick Randolph, Bill Chesnut, Joel Pobar, Dominic and Joseph Cooney, Nick Weinholt, Jeff Alexander, Michael Kleef, Dan Green, Neil Roodyn, John and Athena Pawlowski, Kevin Schuler, Rose Stamell, Geoff Orr, Richard Campbell, Scott Hanselman, Carl Franklin, Rob Farley, Darren Neimke, Peter Ward, Bob Beauchemin, Wally McClure, Kent Tegels, Kevin Kline and Ray Trattles. I hope I haven't missed anyone but I'm sure I will have. For this I apologize in advance.

Special mention must go to my technical editor Chris Wallace, along with Jeff Edman, Kim Turner, and all at Rational Press. Special thanks to Stephen Price for inspiring the Linux cartoon.

My wife Mai has been a wonderful source of support and inspiration throughout and my daughters Kirsty, Andrea and Erin have been a great source of joy. My biggest thanks though needs to go to my mother Joan, who instilled an interest in learning (along with a curious nature) in me and to my late father Jock, who supported us and made my learning possible in the first place.

Contents

Contents

Contents

Part I

Overview

Chapter 1

People, Not Technology

Have you ever been a member of a group and felt like not a single person would notice whether you were there or not? Most of us have. My hope is that after reading this book, if you are running or even just starting a user group or technical community, your group or community won't be like that.

When I first started attending university (too long ago now to admit when), I clearly recall a cartoon in the student newspaper that summed up the situation pretty well. In it, the vice-chancellor (or president) of the university was standing, looking down at a student who looked concerned about something and was saying: "Of course we love you 970-341-2784."

When people decide to start user groups or technical communities, invariably the discussion centers around the technology required to support the group's activities. While using just enough technology is important, this is the wrong place to start.

Communities, whether technical or not, are about people. The best chance you have to build a strong user community is to build a strong group of people who feel like members and who would likely consider each other to be colleagues, or even better, consider each other to be friends.

Many user groups end up becoming a place where events happen but no community surrounds those events. The attendees don't feel any attachment to the groups, which often fail the first time they encounter any problems, or if the initial leader or founder of the group moves on.

In this book, I share the lessons I've learned over many years of organizing and leading technical user communities. The groups I have run are not perfect. They are, however, long-term groups that are very self-sustaining, have a strong core of members, and feel like communities. Every month, I have worked to make them better. Building a technical user community is never "done." It is always a work in progress.

The recommendations in this book are not offered lightly. In most cases, they are the result of my trial and error over many years. They will provide you with a shortcut to building a successful user group or technical user community.

Why Are You Doing This?

One of the first questions you need to stop and consider is why you want to create a technical community at all. Different people have different reasons for doing this. Some common reasons are:

1. A desire to be involved in a project that helps other people.

2. A desire to create a forum where you yourself can learn things.

3. A desire to promote your own commercial offerings.

4. A desire to promote yourself.

Reason #1 is a good altruistic reason and is a good basis for a group or community. People in the community who have not been involved in helping others never seem to understand the old adage that suggests that when you help others, you receive more in return than you provide, yet it's very true.

Unless you are building a technical community around your own commercial offerings and that is spelled out to the members in advance, reason #3 is usually poisonous. The best groups stay very clear of any commercial involvement. This also applies to sponsors. We'll discuss sponsorship in a later chapter, but it's important to note that user groups or communities that are seen by members as predominantly a vehicle for someone to market to them are usually short-lived. I have often seen user groups with good potential completely derailed by conflicting commercial interests within the group.

Groups formed for reason #4 are usually also short-lived. Most leaders will tell you that you can't lead others by simply declaring yourself the leader. (This also applies to managers in companies). You can only lead people who want to be led by you. Ideally, it will be apparent amongst the members of the community who the leader should be.

I'll also declare my bias regarding group leadership at this point. While it might seem wonderfully democratic to have formal group structures with management committees that make decisions, the highest-achieving groups are usually those with an obvious, committed leader who is able to make decisions when they need to be made. In world politics, it is often claimed that the ideal leadership for a country is provided by a benevolent dictator. It is also claimed that the problem with such dictators is that they rarely remain benevolent. The challenge for you in leading a group is to stay focused on the best interests of your group, while trying to emulate some of the traits of a benevolent dictator. Far more can usually be achieved by decisions that are ninety percent correct but which are taken immediately, than by near-perfect decisions taken too late for them to be effective or after the opportunity has passed.

Reason #2 is also very valid. I am endlessly amazed at what I learn by my participation in user groups. For this reason, I also like to attend meetings regardless of the topic. Real gems can pop up without warning. I clearly recall one of my favorite meetings at our local Queensland MSDN User Group around ten years ago. Mike LeVoi was making a presentation on implementing MIDI (Musical Instrument Digital Interface). While it would have been easy to look at that meeting topic and think "I have no interest in that," I attended. It turned out to be one of the most interesting meetings I've ever attended. It wasn't the MIDI part that fascinated me. It was the approach Mike had taken to his user interface and how he had implemented it in Visual Basic.

I constantly assess potential meeting topics on the basis of what I think members would like to learn, but also with an eye to what I would personally like to learn. Fortunately, these areas intersect regularly.

User Groups versus Technical Communities

Much of the discussion in this book relates to user groups that are involved in face-to-face meetings. However, a great deal of the information relates to any form of technical community. In the discussions that follow, I will use the term "user group" to refer specifically to those technical communities that hold face-to-face meetings.

In many countries, it is very difficult to hold regular face-to-face meetings. For example, imagine trying to hold a user group in the middle of a very large city with significant traffic problems, in a sparsely populated island chain, or a location cut off from others because of weather, language, or political restrictions. Members would have to make a huge effort to be able to physically get to the meeting venue and sometimes this just isn't possible. Often, technical communities in some countries work in a combination of online and offline modes.

My favorite user group in the whole world is a .NET developer group in Korea that has over 170,000 members in an online community. Street traffic is slow but network connections are fast. It holds a face-to-face meeting only annually. At the meeting, they have around eight to ten thousand attendees (yes, read those numbers carefully). The meeting is held in the Olympic soccer stadium in Seoul and looks like a rock concert. The photo below shows a recent annual meeting.

Figure 1.1: Korean .NET User Group (Photo courtesy of Microsoft Regional Director Dong-Bum Lee).

While user groups are usually geographically limited, online technical communities can easily span the globe. There are substantial challenges involved with these communities too. It is really difficult to build any community feeling amongst such widespread members, yet in the best online communities, this still occurs. In addition, widespread cultural differences can easily create tensions. Anyone who has been involved in an online community can usually tell tales of the last "flame war" they have experienced.

For example, over many years I have been involved in the MCT (Microsoft Certified Trainer) newsgroups. This community involves around ten thousand professionals from around the world. After many years of dealing with people online, a sense of friendship (and a sense of humor) develops amongst the trainers. The beauty of this is seen whenever I meet other trainers face-to-face. Even though I may never have met them before (in person), when I eventually have the good luck to do so, they feel like long lost friends and treat me the way they would treat an old friend.

How Technical Communities Differ from Other Communities

This book shows that technical communities have more in common with other types of community than differences. "Community" is the key word.

First, technical communities tend to relate to members' work. Because of this, commercial interests can (and often do) impact the ability to share ideas and assist others. For example, most user groups find it very difficult to get members to present details of what they have been developing at their workplaces. This is understandable because competitors may well be in the audience. It is also likely that the organizations they work for will have rules and regulations covering disclosure of intellectual property outside the organization.

Commercial organizations may also be very keen for their employees to make presentations at user groups, because they see this as a direct form of advertising for the company. My experience is that as soon as group members feel they are being subjected to advertising, they quickly lose interest in the group. Whenever I am approached by a prospective speaker that I don't know, the first thing I do is make it very clear to them that the group is not a vehicle for advertising.

Second, members of technical communities tend to be very proud of their own technical achievements. It takes a certain type of person to be prepared to present details of their technical work and be prepared for open and honest criticism (constructive or not) from an audience. Those who are prepared to do so usually learn the most from the experience. I have regularly seen members present at one of our meetings, spend a long time discussing the pros and cons of their approach in detail, and leave the meeting having learned more than the attendees.

Third, members of technical communities seem to feel far more protective of their own technical decisions than those in other forms of communities. The quickest way to start an endless discussion in a technical community is to ask which development language is the best to use or to ask for advice on coding standards. Discussions with near-religious convictions tend to immediately spring up, with each participant dogmatically entrenched in the defense of their own methodologies or languages. I have come across people (commonly called *trolls* in the newsgroups) who start these discussions as a form of sport. They wait for a quiet moment and then bait the members of the group with an innocent-looking question along these lines, just to watch the outcome. If nothing else, members of technical communities display a great deal of passion in these areas.

Summary

This chapter stressed that the key focus on building a user group or technical community needs to be on people, not on the technology involved in running the group or community.

We discussed the most common reasons for wanting to start or take over the running of such communities. The best reasons usually involve a desire to be involved in a project that helps other people, and a desire to create a forum where you yourself can learn things. Technical communities created from a desire to promote yourself or a commercial offering are usually unsuccessful.

Finally, we looked at the difference between online and offline communities, and how technical communities differ from other types of communities.

Chapter 2

Something for Everyone

In this chapter, we discuss the importance of providing the best experience you can for every single member attending any user group meeting. Each and every meeting is important.

Every Member Needs Value at Every Meeting

Think back to the first time you attended any form of community meeting or group. How much time and effort did you spend thinking about going and planning to do so? If you are like most people, you spent quite a bit of time on that. You went to the trouble to find out about the group, perhaps spent some time joining a mailing list or notification list and providing some of your details to the organizers. Each and every time you attended the group, you also expended quite a bit of effort. You also decided that attending the group was more important than all the other things you could have done instead. This means that even before you walked in the door the first time, you have made a substantial commitment to the group.

Next, as a group leader, think about how much effort you are likely to spend attracting new members to your community. It's likely you will spend quite a bit of time on this too. You may well be involved in organizing speakers, ensuring that catering happens, dealing with venue issues, notifying members about the meeting, and dealing with RSVPs, unexpected changes and the like, while fitting this into your own busy life. Even if you organize an online community rather than a face-to-face one, the effort is no smaller.

Given the amount of effort put in by both the new attendee and the organizers, how much of that effort would you like to see thrown away? Hopefully, the answer is "none." Yet this is precisely what happens with most new attendees in most groups. I believe the key reason is that meetings need to offer every member something of value, every time they make the effort to attend.

Strategy 1: Avoid Single Topic Meetings

The first strategy is to avoid single-topic meetings. My favorite meeting mix is to have around 30 minutes of introductory-level material followed by about an hour of more advanced material. Ideally, the two parts of the meeting cover different topics entirely.

Strategy 2: Avoid Increasing Depth

A common problem in technical user communities is that after a period of time, the topics of discussion tend to become quite advanced and narrow in focus. It is also quite common for advanced groups to endlessly dwell on bleeding-edge technology. While this might be fine for the core members of the group who have attended each and every introductory meeting, it is not fine for most members.

Strategy 3: Some Repetition is OK

As an organizer, it is easy to fall into the trap where you feel like everyone has seen all the introductory-level topics before. In fact, you'll start to avoid any topic that has ever been covered at the group at any time in the past. This is a mistake. While you may have attended almost every meeting, most members will not have. There will be topics they wish they had been able to attend but their lives intervened in some way to stop them.

For example, one SQL Server user group I have been involved with started discussing SQL Server 2005 topics in June 2004. The product was not released until November 2005 and not widely implemented till well after that. So, by the time the product was released, most key topics related to the new product had already been dealt with in detail. Imagine how this would have struck a new member joining in November 2005 when the product had just been released. The day they joined the group, they would find they had already missed all the key information on the new product. They would likely struggle to follow any of the discussion where there was already a great deal of assumed knowledge. It is very important to constantly revisit old ground.

Participation is the Key (No Statues)

At an INETA Worldwide Conference in Malaysia in 2005, one topic that really caught my eye was a session on recruiting volunteers. The lady making the presentation noted that the key reason people don't volunteer is that they haven't been asked. While it might often seem difficult to get group members to take on volunteer roles, they will never do so if they aren't asked.

An aspect I thought was missing from her session was that volunteers also need to share your vision for where your community is going. Apart from remembering to ask people to help, it is critical for them to want to achieve the result you are seeking from them. In addition, the volunteers need to feel that their contribution really matters.

You need to clearly enunciate two things to prospective volunteers: why your goals are important and how their individual contribution helps get you there.

It is very important to delegate tasks to your volunteers on a regular basis. While you may feel like you have boundless energy to invest in your community, it will be a far stronger community if there are a number of people who can step in to your roles when needed. Our local Microsoft DPE (Developer and Platform Evangelism) team member Charles Sterling told me he thinks one of the strengths of our developer community is that *"when Greg isn't there, one of his lieutenants steps in to do the job."* This was in contrast to another community that has a strong leader and normally functions well but flounders when that leader isn't present. I had not considered how important that was until he mentioned it, but it was an insightful observation. Members who feel they have an active and ongoing role in your community will become the mainstay of the community.

While you may have explained to a volunteer how his or her contribution is important at the time you asked them to help, it is critical to continually reinforce their value to them, particularly if the task is a long-running one. Everyone wants to feel valued. Volunteers who are doing long-running tasks and don't feel recognized can become jaded, disillusioned, and disinterested. Some could also become disruptive. In many management courses I have attended, the point is made that staff who feel valued and who receive constant reinforcement usually rate this as more important than other conditions, including salary. Where unpaid volunteer efforts are involved, this is critical.

Volunteers should be asked to do specific tasks. The more specific the task, the more likely it can be defined, executed, and reviewed. Tasks may be short or long term. Some volunteers want to be involved but do not want to take on a never-ending assignment. Other volunteers may be quite comfortable in assuming areas of responsibility that are of long duration.

Networking Opportunities

Networking opportunities are crucial to many of your community members. In groups that meet face-to-face, a common mistake is to provide so much content for the members to consume that the opportunities for them to network are limited. By networking, I'm referring to meeting other community members, discussing areas of common interest, and perhaps sharing work and other opportunities with each other.

I made this mistake at our first CodeCampOz event in April 2005 (organized in conjunction with ASP.NET MVP and Readify colleague Mitch Denny). While it was deemed a very successful event, I was so keen to have masses of content for attendees that the schedule I came up with (I'm letting Mitch off the hook here) really didn't have enough time for attendees to just talk to each other. Furthermore, although most were in the town of Wagga Wagga over the weekend, I didn't suggest any activities or get-togethers outside the formal event's content.

At CodeCampOz in April 2006, we scheduled a couple of breaks during the day, Charles Sturt University graciously provided a wine and cheese tasting session, and while we didn't have a dinner as a formal part of the event, we recommended where attendees might get together on each of the nights. This worked very well. Around one third of the attendees came to the nominated restaurant on the first night and over two thirds of the attendees came to the other nominated restaurant on the second night. From the feedback we received from attendees, those evening activities (while unofficial) were rated very highly, as were the improved chances to network during the days. Clearly this can be overdone and it is important to realize that many attendees are keen to see a large amount of content.

Another aspect of networking is the relationship with university students and other new entrants to the industry. Given the accelerated rate of technological change in the community as a whole, it is important to realize that today's students can quickly become influential members of the community. I predominantly work in the IT industry and often tell people in that industry that they need to be prepared for around eighty percent of what they know today to be fairly valueless within four years. Detailed technical knowledge has a short life in the IT industry. This means that within a few years newcomers to the industry can be as knowledgeable as anyone else on certain topics.

Growing Friendships and Loyalty

Regardless of the type of technical community you are building or managing, it is important that your members come to regard each other as friends. They will then feel very different about attending functions or contributing online because they feel at ease. Every time I think about the sort of community I like to build, I'm reminded of the television show *Cheers* and the theme song that said: "you wanna go where everybody knows your name." This is so very true and a large part of human nature. Everyone likes to belong and to feel comfortable in their surroundings.

A common problem that can occur in many technical user communities is that members might see each other as competitors and not be prepared to share information willingly. This is far less likely to be a problem if they see the other member as a friend. Trust takes time to build. Members who come to see each other as friends and trust each other will usually find they are better off in the long run, because they will gain just as much as they offer. I have seen countless examples of user group members who gained significant commercial benefit directly from other members—people they might initially consider to be competitors—because a level of friendship and trust has developed.

Along with friendship within the group comes loyalty to the group. People who feel they belong and who feel comfortable and at ease within a group will become the strongest contributors. They will also feel a strong association with the group, no matter how informal the association really is. Friends will also feel more personally responsible when volunteering for tasks and supporting their community in other activities. For example, the QMSDN user group I manage has many members who would describe themselves as members, who would offer to help out whenever a volunteer is needed (and often at short notice), who would help integrate newcomers to the group, who reliably attend meetings, and who would participate in inter-group friendly rivalry and banter. Yet, the group has no formal concept of membership, apart from being listed on a meeting notification e-mail list.

In certain cultures, one way of building group loyalty is to foster some form of friendly rivalry between your group or community and other similar ones in other areas. As an example, over the next year I hope to engender a sense of fun competition between my groups and those in other states. In Australian culture, that will also involve a degree of friendly tongue-in-cheek joking, which may at first glance seem competitive, but which in reality creates a bond between groups with similar interests.

Summary

This chapter discussed the effort that members make to attend a group meeting and the efforts of group leaders to prepare for one. Those efforts are wasted if newcomers do not have a good experience when they attend a meeting or join a group. We discussed strategies for ensuring that every member gains something each time they participate: avoid single topic meetings, do not let topics become too narrow or advanced in focus at the expense of introductory material, and realize that it's fine to allow some repetition of topics.

Participation is very important. Make sure that volunteers share the overall vision of where the community is going, and that their tasks are specific enough to be clearly defined, executed, and reviewed. Always make certain that volunteer efforts are recognized and appreciated.

Do not provide so much content for your members to consume that they lose the chance to network. Members need to meet each other, discuss areas of common interest, and share opportunities.

Friendships and loyalty to the group can be built without being based on formal structures. Members who feel at ease with each other will become the strongest contributors.

Chapter 3

Finding Speakers

I endlessly hear about user groups that cannot seem to gain traction because they cannot ever seem to find good speakers. In this chapter I will show you why they are looking in the wrong places for speakers.

First Impressions Matter

While friendships and feelings of loyalty will help retain members, groups that have face-to-face meetings usually need someone who makes a presentation on a topic of interest. The ongoing quality of these presentations will have a great effect on your ability to retain group members and keep them interested.

The very first meeting that your group holds will often have a great effect on how quickly your group becomes a success. Similar to many other things in life, the first impressions of your group meetings really do matter. Word of mouth can be a powerful advertising tool for you, but poor comments can be poison. So, it is important to try to have a great first impression.

I would suggest that for your very first meeting, you take the time to find a stellar speaker if at all possible. You will be surprised how many people will be prepared to help you, if you only think to ask them. I am the host of a podcast called SQL Down Under (www. sqldownunder.com). In the podcast (audio show), I interview people I think are notable or important in the SQL Server space. While I was at the PASS (Professional Association of SQL Server) conference in Dallas in 2005, I had the honor to meet and spend some time with Dr. Jim Gray. He had been one of my heroes while I was first learning about databases. Dr. Gray is described as a "distinguished engineer" at Microsoft. He is a legend in the database industry. On my return to Australia it occurred to me that he would be a wonderful guest on the podcast. Even though I presumed he'd be way too busy to participate, I contacted him, reminded him of our meeting in Dallas and asked him to take part. To my surprise, he managed to fit it into his schedule and was happy to help. The show I recorded with him has been one of the most popular shows I have ever done.

Even if it means potentially delaying your first meeting, I would strongly suggest finding a great guest speaker for that first meeting. There are three great outcomes from this. First, the quality of the presentation at the meeting is very likely to be high. Second, you are much more likely to get greater coverage about your meeting both before and after it takes place. The speaker is also likely to be able to help with spreading the word about his/her appearance at your group. Lastly, an apparent association with a well-known identity instantly provides a sense of additional legitimacy to your group.

Ongoing Speaker Quality is Important

While having a great first meeting for your group is very important, you also need to be concerned about providing great ongoing value to your members. There's an old saying in the movie industry that you're "only as good as your last movie." While running a user group isn't quite so brutal and you'll get some forgiveness for meetings that aren't spectacular, any member who doesn't find anything useful over a few consecutive meetings is unlikely to continue attending.

In sales and marketing training, perceived wisdom is that it's about ten times harder to get a new customer than it is to keep an existing one, but regaining one you've lost is about a hundred times harder again. If someone takes the time to come along to one of your meetings, you must strive to make sure they get some value each and every time that they attend.

In the next section, I discuss techniques for developing new speakers. Invariably, this means that you will have meetings at which you are trying out new speakers, and at such times you should strongly consider having a very experienced speaker also present at the same meeting. While this may seem a bit daunting for the inexperienced speaker, it ensures that attendees get good value from attending, regardless of what the inexperienced speaker is like.

Another piece of old wisdom is to "not put all your eggs in one basket." Having more than one speaker at each meeting (and preferably more than one topic) also helps avoid the chance that a meeting will be a dud.

Techniques for "Growing" New Speakers

One of the most common complaints I hear from user groups is that they can't find enough good speakers for their meetings. When I look around the country, I see three types of groups. One type of group can never seem to find enough speakers and is endlessly cancelling or changing meetings. The next type has the leader of the group speaking almost all the time. The third type of group has many speakers available, is in control of its own destiny, and regularly provides speakers to other groups. It is important to try to move your group into this third category.

"Growing" or developing new speakers takes time, but it is one of the most worthwhile and rewarding chores you will undertake as a user group leader. The effort you put into this will be returned to you many times over. So how do you start doing it?

If you have made lots of presentations in your life, think back to a time when you hadn't; otherwise think about how you feel about presenting now. If you were a member of a user group, think about your reaction the first time the leader came up and said, "Hi Tom, I know you've been working on some interesting things at work lately. Would you be prepared to come and talk about it at the meeting next month? Would you be able to cover the hour and a half ok?" Most people would immediately shy away from this. Yet this is exactly the approach I see user group leaders taking when trying to get new speakers for their groups.

There are a number of reasons why group members would be hesitant about talking:

1. They are not used to public speaking at all and are nervous about it.

2. They are not confident of their technical ability—at least not confident enough to have it critiqued by their peers for an hour and a half.

3. They are not sure they could entertain a crowd for that long.

4. Much of the material they may have that is suitable for presentation is actually company confidential in some way.

5. They are not used to structuring a presentation.

If you want the person to become a presenter, you need to overcome these issues. I have found the best way to do this is to ask them to do something much simpler. If instead of asking them to present an interesting topic for an hour and a half, consider the response you'd get if you asked in this manner:

"Hi Tom, I've been thinking that a short talk on XXXX would help out the newcomers to the group. Mary's going to do a pretty deep session on YYYY in three month's time and I think it'd be a great addition to that meeting. It would certainly help the less experienced people get something worthwhile out of the meeting, and a few of the old timers might learn a few things as well. How would you feel about talking for, say, 20 minutes on that in three months time?"

Having done this many times, I know that the response is usually "yes." The keys to making this work are:

1. Pick an introductory-level topic that the member is already confident about.

2. Give them plenty of time to prepare.

3. Keep their session short enough that they don't see the preparation as an onerous task and that they know they could not possibly run out of material to cover.

4. Have the topic general enough that they will not need to draw on any company confidential material.

This approach has many advantages. Once a member has done this once or twice, they might find they actually like presenting. At least they might be reasonably comfortable doing short presentations. If they get a taste for it, they will become your main presenters over time.

Don't be concerned about having these introductory-level topics regularly either. They fit very nicely with my earlier advice on making sure you have something for everyone at each meeting. Many, many times I have seen introductory-level presentations at user groups where almost every experienced person in the room has picked up some new information. This is bound to happen if you have an experienced person who takes an introductory-level topic and spends some time researching it while preparing for their talk. Most people simply don't tend to read and re-read introductory-level material, yet it often changes or becomes extended. Even experienced people aren't experts in everything.

It is important to not push members to present information that their companies might not be comfortable with them presenting. You want them to have a great experience the first time they speak and certainly don't want them feeling uncomfortable about having revealed a little too much private company information. Having them present on basic topics gets around this. When the speaker is more experienced, they will know how to limit their exposure of company information to an acceptable level. Speak with them about this as they prepare, so that there are no surprises at delivery time.

Providing the new speaker with plenty of time to prepare is also vital. You do not want to give the impression that you are asking them to speak because you have run out of other speakers. Allowing them plenty of time helps with that perception. You need them to feel special for being asked to speak, not that they are helping you out because you are desperate. Many times, user group leaders are scrambling to fill speaking positions days or a few weeks before a meeting. It takes a user group leader just as much time to prepare for a speaker three months ahead as it does one month ahead; however, the leader will sleep so much better for those three months.

While a new speaker is presenting, I would also suggest positioning yourself in the room so that you can see all of the audience. My personal preference is to be either at the back of the room or right at the front of the room, on the side. Make it very clear (privately) to the speaker that you are on hand for any help that's needed, particularly with any audio-visual equipment issues. Be prepared to help out if the speaker gets stuck in any way, but do so by assisting the conversation. Do not take over the conversation, because that would be either demoralizing or demeaning and you stand a good chance of losing your new speaker.

After a speaker's first presentation, positive reinforcement of what they did well is most important. Suggestions on how they might have improved the talk should be made, but try to keep these comments focused on specific things the speaker might have done in the talk they just gave, rather than just making general comments. Hopefully, the speaker will then suggest that they'd like to tackle another topic another day. If not, don't push this. Leave it a few months before having another chat with them. If making presentations works out for them, they will usually let you know, and will eventually progress to presenting more complex sessions.

Keeping Speakers Interested

Along with the need to grow new speakers, you need to keep your existing speakers willing to come back time and time again. I was talking with a very experienced speaker recently and he asked (rhetorically), "Why do we do it?" He was referring to preparing and presenting session after session, usually for free.

In some cases, indirect business or professional promotion might be an aim, but many people also just like helping others and feel they get as much back as they provide. While you may not be in a position to provide monetary rewards for those who offer to speak at your group, there are some things you can do to keep their interest peaked.

Recognition is vital. Obviously, you must thank the speakers when they have presented. Do so informally but also formally in writing (e-mail) and make sure to copy those who may have introduced your speaker to you and those who may be influenced by your recommendation. Other forms of recognition are important too. When opportunities arise that could benefit members of your group, such as free attendance at seminars or conferences or free samples provided by sponsors, etc., the members who are willing to speak and share their knowledge with others should be near the top of the list for consideration. The only members I place higher on my list to receive "freebies" are those I know are in genuine hardship for some reason. Make sure to announce your upcoming and past speakers on your user group Web site and newsletters.

You can also give recognition outside your group. Speak regularly to other group leaders, even if they are in other areas of the country. Promote your speakers to those other groups and to key suppliers and sponsors. I get a great sense of pride seeing former (and current) group members spreading their wings and speaking at national or international conferences, particularly if I also remember their first speaking efforts at one of our groups. You may become aware of job opportunities or client requests for specific experiences that your speakers have shown you. Recommending these talented people, with their permission, will always be rewarding to you, them, and the client.

Summary

This chapter stressed that having a big impact in your first meeting is vital. Having an outstanding speaker for your first meeting will help to do this.

I described how you need to ensure the ongoing quality of the presentations in your meetings. Members who don't find anything useful over a few consecutive meetings are unlikely to return. Remember, it's harder to find new members than it is to retain existing ones.

It is important to develop new speakers from amongst your group members. We discussed some typical reasons why members might hesitate to become speakers and how to overcome these obstacles.

Finally, we looked at various ways to provide recognition to your speakers, to keep them interested enough to come back for more.

"I knew this was a bad idea."

Did you know?

It's worth warning new speakers that they might find presenting to be physically draining. It's usually after my better presentations that I feel most exhausted. New speakers often mistake this for nervous tension but it's more an indication of how much effort you have put into the presentation. Presenting can be hard work!

Chapter 4

Tried and True

Getting a community started is an important first step. Keeping the community going is just as important. In this chapter, we'll look at techniques for sustaining a thriving community.

Consistency Matters

There's an old saying in the movie industry that you're only as good as your last movie. While running a technical user community is not quite as cut-throat as that, it is very important to maintain a significant degree of consistency.

For groups that meet face-to-face, a regular meeting schedule is crucial. I have seen a variety of groups over the years and those that seem to have a real sense of community also tend to have a regular schedule.

I like to see groups meet at least monthly and have a regular pattern of meetings, such as the second Tuesday or the third Thursday of the month. For more regular meetings, a schedule based on fortnights seems to work well, such as every second Wednesday.

The beauty of such schedules is that over time, several forces start to work in your favor. First, members are able to easily remember the schedule. This means that when a spouse (or significant other) asks if anything is happening on Wednesday night, they might at least think, "Ah Wednesday, is that one of my user group nights?" Most people will simply plan around regular dates if they are easy to remember, the same way they will around sporting events.

Second, you are much more likely to be able to secure a venue where you have a regular schedule. People that organize venues tend to really appreciate consistency regarding time. Of course, you will often be looking to use the venue at little or low cost and often somewhat as a favor, so it is important to not cause heartache or difficulty for those providing the venue to you. Consistency in timing is an important step in this.

Third, when your schedule becomes known by people outside your group, they are more likely to be able to help you. You may well start to receive offers for speakers more reliably. For example, if another user group leader is in your town and they know your schedule well in advance, they might choose to come along to your group and/or offer to present for you. In fact, given a choice of dates, they might even schedule their own trip to coincide with your user group meeting.

Fourth, when your schedules are known well in advance, you will find that members will plan their other activities around your schedule. For example, a member joining an adult-education class or a sporting group might well choose to make sure your meeting times are free if the other activity offers a choice of times.

Fifth, members are much more likely to actually arrive at your meetings if they know a consistent schedule. You want to get them to the point where they will remember your meeting when they are making decisions about what to do next. Many will think, "Time to go home. Do I need to do anything on the way? It's Thursday. Ah, it's the fourth Thursday. That's right, I have a meeting tonight." User group leaders have told me that once they have established a consistent day and time, any variation due to holidays or special needs will likely result in lowered attendance and general confusion. When you need to choose an alternate day or time, do so with great care and ample notification.

There is no right or wrong time of the day for a meeting. I have traditionally been involved in night-time meetings but I have also seen cities where lunch time events are the norm. I have also seen breakfast meetings work well even in the same town where I normally ran evening meetings. The key is that you will likely attract a different group of attendees at different times of the day. It won't be a better or worse group, just a different group, even though some will overlap.

Once again however, keeping the time of the day consistent is just as important as keeping the date schedule consistent. I should also close this section by noting that I am not referring to special events. They can be at very different schedules to your "normal" schedule. In fact, they are much more likely to be treated as special if they are.

Don't Stray Too Far from What Works

I often hear user group leaders complaining that other groups are opening up in "their area." Do not be concerned about this. It can be a surprisingly good thing.

Have you ever seen a location where a fast-food shop opens up and then soon after, others open up almost beside them? Simple logic would suggest that they would all suffer, but simple logic does not apply. It is not a zero-sum game. It is often the case that all the shops end up doing better than if they were situated on their own. This is because when customers want fast-food, they will start to head to that area before they even really think about what they want. They will just know that's where they want to be.

I have found two things in relation to this.

The first is that helping other user groups get started and helping them with speakers has never diminished any of the groups I've been involved with. If anything, it has always tended to improve or enhance them in some way.

The second is that user groups are not a zero-sum game either. Each successful group will tend to gain a following that is appropriate for the group and this will often be a very different following from another group in the same area. There will be some aspect of the group's culture and behavior that just "works" for the members. As an example, some developer groups are very hobbyist in nature. They might mostly have members making presentations on their own work and meet in the evening after work. Another group in the same city might aspire to higher-quality presentations, central business district locations, and lunch time meetings. It isn't likely that these two groups will really detract from each other. If they share resources and ideas though, they may end up helping each other. Some groups also fear being split into multiple groups. Don't concern yourself about this as a problem. Several specialized groups might serve a membership better than a broader generalized group. Each user group brings special traits to the table to benefit the total community.

If members keep coming back to a group, there must be something that just works for them about that group. The lesson to be learned from this is: Don't stray too far from what you already know works. If you keep changing the culture of your group, you will never build a solid membership. Each group member needs to feel like they belong in the group, so don't change the fundamentals that they liked about the group in the first place.

Periodically and rather formally, look at your user group and determine if specialty sub-groups or special interest groups become worthy of their own status as a standalone user group, or whether they would be better served as a recognized part of your larger group.

If you are holding face-to-face meetings, try to keep the format of your meetings similar and predictable. Don't make them boring, but find a format that works and stick to it. One format that works well is this:

- ▶ Start with the group leader discussing any newsworthy items.

- ▶ Lead into finding out about new members or attendees and getting them to introduce themselves.

- ▶ Introduce the first speaker and let them cover the intro-level topic.

- ▶ While the second speaker sets up, use the break to discuss any tips or tricks that anyone attending has uncovered lately (keep this section short and precise).

- ▶ Introduce the main speaker and let them cover the main topic.

- ▶ The user group leader covers any important reminders, particularly those that require action from attendees.

Rather than having an unstructured break, refer to the break between speakers as "a networking break"—this gives credibility to your members' personal and professional networking time. You may also name and specify a time prior to the start of each meeting as networking time. The point is to not waste any of your members' time—you must provide structure, but maintain the freedom of exchange.

Keep Your Content Topical

A key role for a user group leader is deciding what appropriate and interesting content to offer to members at meetings. As with most things, there is no strict right or wrong way to do this. However, I have learned a number of lessons in this area.

Avoid advertising that is cloaked as a technical presentation. If you are having someone from a vendor organization make a presentation, make it very clear to them beforehand what you expect in this regard. Do not leave this discussion until just before they start presenting either. It may be way too late for them to alter their material appropriately. Most members of technical communities are already bombarded with advertising everywhere they look. I was watching a new movie recently when it struck me just how much product placement is now happening even in quite serious movies. While it is somewhat subtle, even that starts to be very distracting. Don't make your meetings into another source of this. If you decide to accept a sponsorship from someone who requires a period of time to promote their products or services, make sure that the advertising time is clearly spelled out for your members and not hidden in a technical presentation. If the sponsor wants more time, strictly enforce that any additional time must be spent on topics that all members will find useful, not just those using the sponsor's products.

Make sure you regularly cover intro-level topics for part of your meetings. Ideally, most basics should be covered over the period of each year, so that a new member will have the opportunity to see the most important intro-level topics within a year of starting to attend.

Make sure you have a balance of super-technical topics. Some groups feel very proud of just how deeply they cover material all the time. They don't tend to have many members and new members often don't return. Unless your group is called the "super gung-ho ninja guerilla take-no-prisoners group," don't act like one. Keep a balance.

Most technical communities are based around specific technologies. The user group leader needs to be keenly aware of directions that the vendors of the technologies are taking. Those vendors often have road maps that clearly indicate this, long before they get there. For example, I have been involved with a number of user groups based around Microsoft development tools. Microsoft publishes all sorts of details about upcoming product directions. Other companies do the same thing. It is important that in your planning, you take into account these directions As a user group leader, your members are looking for you to help guide them by presenting topic areas that are important for them to know about. They also like to know what's coming in the near future.

Often, companies like Microsoft also have marketing plans that they are willing to share with partners. These indicate what will be particularly promoted in which periods. You can maximize the interest in your group meetings if you try to ensure that your meetings target the right topics at about the right time. This can help you work out what future topics you would like to see covered, to find appropriate speakers for those topics or, preferably, to develop one of the members of your group to be that speaker. It is very likely in any technical community that you will already have a group member with a keen interest in the upcoming area. It is your role to find that person and to encourage them.

Summary

This chapter focused on communities that hold face-to-face meetings and discussed the importance of consistency in all aspects of a user group. This includes meeting times, meeting schedule, and basic meeting formats. A sample meeting format was discussed.

We also discussed the idea that user groups tend to have a culture that draws members. It is important to avoid changing that culture on an ad-hoc basis. If you keep changing the culture of your group, you will never build a solid membership.

Lastly, we discussed methods for keeping meetings topical. Avoid advertising that is cloaked as a technical presentation. Make sure you balance intro-level topics with very advanced topics. Maintain an awareness of where technology vendors are heading in their product development. Members like to know what's coming in the near future, and it will let you find appropriate speakers in advance, or groom members to present on those new developments when the time comes.

"Is this the LINUX group?"

Part II

Starting and Growing User Groups

Chapter 5

Pizza Does Not Define a User Group

In this chapter, we'll see that a user group isn't defined only by the refreshments that are provided at the meeting, but we'll also discuss why they might help. We'll look at some techniques for keeping interest levels high.

Pizza Isn't Everything

There seems to be a belief that user groups are all about pizza and beer. Generally, I believe it really doesn't matter.

At the QMSDN user group many years ago we used to ask members to contribute $5 per meeting to the cost of the refreshments This worked very well for a very long time. In July 2000, Australia introduced a goods and services tax. This made it very important for people to collect invoices known as "tax invoices." We found that user group members who worked for either the government or large corporations started asking for tax invoices for their $5. This was because the member was being reimbursed for the $5 by their employer and now the employer wanted the tax invoice.

Tax invoices could only be issued by organizations that were registered with our taxation office. For us to start issuing tax invoices, we would have needed to have incorporated the user group, have annual general meetings, complete monthly tax business activity statements, etc.

We decided that that was all just too hard. We decided to simply stop having pizza and drinks. At the time, we hadn't been providing beer anyway. We heard many predictions that attendance at meetings would fall off. After several months of operating without refreshments, it became very clear to us that attendance had not changed in any way.

While refreshments might make the meetings more pleasant for attendees, the lack of it did not seem to stop them attending.

The real beauty of having some level of refreshments is that it helps with networking opportunities for members. At our meetings, pizza and drinks were used before the meeting and most members found this time very fruitful for their personal networking. Eating and drinking tend to stimulate conversations, much the same way that people often use meals as social gatherings or the way that business people hold meetings over lunches or dinners.

So, while a user group isn't defined by pizza and beer, I'd suggest that some form of refreshments is important during networking sessions. For the QMSDN user group, after a few months of meeting without refreshments, our local Microsoft office graciously agreed to provide some refreshments for our meetings. I think they were impressed by the commitment to continue without the refreshments. This gave us the best of both worlds where we had refreshments in place but still didn't have to deal with the issues surrounding incorporation.

Refreshments like light dinners or snacks also serve another real and serious purpose— and that is not just to have sponsors pay for dinner! Let's say your user group meetings are in the evenings during the work week, like many meetings are. When your members are leaving work, they are hungry and they are deciding "should I go to my user group meeting or go eat dinner at home?" You want them to make the right decision. Of course, that is to go to your user group meeting! In many locations, it is unlikely that your members will have enough time to eat before navigating traffic to get to your meeting. Once they go home, you may have lost the opportunity to get them to attend your meeting. They know that without food at the meeting, they are going to be hungry all night until well after they leave.

You want your members to know that they can get some food to help them overcome hunger for the evening. When you provide them something to eat, the lack of food does not become a deterrent and negatively influence their decision to come to your meeting. You need to wipe away any negative about deciding not to attend and being hungry during the meeting. Refreshments handle that for you.

On the subject of refreshments, I'm also heartened by the healthy options pushed by some user groups. A number of groups are starting to use things like sushi or healthier subs and avoiding fatty or fried foods. If that is an option for your group, it could well be worth pursuing.

Swag is Important

A fellow Microsoft MVP and friend Nick Randolph and I were at an INETA conference in Bangkok in 2003. At the end of the conference, the hosts graciously gave us some presents, some of which had value or significance. However, Nick and I could both be found at a table full of odds and ends, much more interested in gathering up numbers of small items such as shirts, executive toys (like squeeze balls), and books. We were both quite happy to have our return luggage loaded down with these sorts of items. As a user group leader, Nick understood, the same way I did, that having lots of little pieces of *swag* to give away when we got back to our groups was pure gold. This can add significantly to making the meetings fun. The value of the item isn't the issue.

Competitions Work

Consider how much work you would be prepared to do for me if the total compensation I was providing to you was a mouse pad. Most people would barely even take the time to discuss such a task.

Years ago, I was very impressed by the California Avocado Web site (www.avocado.org). On the site, there was a competition area where you could win a "Cali the surfing avocado" mouse pad. To win one, you had to answer a number of questions about avocados and if you got them all correct, you were in the running to win one of the mouse pads. Even after answering all the questions correctly, you still weren't assured of even winning a mouse pad. I watched two IT professionals spend many, many hours reading pages of information about avocados so they could answer the questions correctly each day. Then, every morning, they would each connect to the Web site and answer questions until they got them all correct and hoped that that was the day that they would win a Cali mouse pad.

Now you may be asking yourself who in their right mind would waste that amount of time to win a mouse pad, but watching this taught me a very specific lesson about the value of competitions. The issue was not the value of the mouse pad. It was that no one else that they knew had one. And they wanted one. I never underestimate the effort that people will expend competitively. All it takes is a cute outcome and someone to compete with.

For many years in the 1980s, I worked for Hewlett Packard. One of the things I loved about the company was the way they liked to see staff members "dabbling" and trying out new things. What impressed me more is that they didn't mind if several teams of people were dabbling on basically the same thing. They believed they got a better "thing" out of it.

When I was working as a lecturer at Queensland University of Technology, I applied some of this logic very successfully in managing final year student projects. I found I got the best outcomes on projects when I had two teams of people working on the same topic. During my meetings with each team, I would give each team hints about things the other team was working on. Invariably, this would push each team to even greater heights as they tried to outdo each other.

People who study time and motion and organizational behavior seem to feel that having two groups of people working on the same thing is a waste of effort. However, I have found that that isn't the case. I found I got better results from two teams of two people each than I got from one team of four or five people, every time.

Many technical people thrive on competition. Non-technical people often do not understand why technical people will spend enormous time and effort on something, for very little outcome. But it is how many truly technical people work. The prize in the end is not the issue—the challenge is what matters.

Also, it is important to realize the role that swag can play in competition. As I've mentioned, not all competitions need to have valuable outcomes. A small but "cool" piece of swag can often be much more highly valued than an expensive prize. I'll give two examples.

The first example of this relates to one trivia night I attended many years ago with my extended family. This was a night where groups of people sit at tables and try to answer questions as a group. Each table tries to outdo the other tables. On the night in question, there were some truly remarkable prizes on offer. However, the thing that caught my eye and my brother-in-law's eye was a simple poster. Compass was an airline that appeared for a while in Australia, went broke and then was resurrected, only to go broke and disappear again. The poster was a simple advertising poster showing one of their airliners. Being both keenly interested in aircraft, we wanted the poster. It was cute and we didn't know anyone who had one. That evening our team ended in first place. We were given a choice of prizes. Much to the dismay of the organizers and most people in the room, we didn't select any of the expensive items. We chose the "worthless" Compass poster.

As a final example of the value of competitive spirit amongst technical people, Microsoft recently produced a number of small rubbery figurines. They started with one called "Nine Guy" and later we saw "Tablet PC Guy," "MSDN Webcast Guy," "SQL Server Girl," and so on. Because they were relatively uncommon, particularly in my country, having one or more was seen as some sort of "badge of honor." I have seen people go to extraordinary lengths to try to get hold of these, particularly to collect a complete set of them. I'm sure that people outside the industry would look at one of these small rubbery toys and wonder how the need to obtain one could drive a technical person to lengths way beyond what a substantial salary could do. This is the energy that needs to be harnessed in your community.

Periodic Events Galvanize Assistance

Even if your community is humming along very well, meeting regularly (if that's appropriate for you) and acting very consistently and reliably, sometimes something more is needed to keep rekindling enthusiasm.

It seems important to have any community engage in a "big picture" event or task every so often. This is very important for building team spirit. While volunteers can give their time to an ongoing cause reliably, a periodic event or task can refocus and galvanize their level of assistance. Such events can cause a large boost in activity levels from existing volunteers and drive those who do not regularly help out to make a special effort.

In each country or community, there will be something special that appeals to members. In Australia, we have a fairly quirky sense of humor and I find the best efforts somehow involve this off-beat nature. In the events I am involved with, I try to take advantage of this in some way. As an aside, I've noticed that some of the best entrepreneurs understand this well. An example of odd Australian humor is that people with red hair are traditionally given the nickname "blue." Richard Branson introduced Virgin Airlines into Australia and held a competition to find a name for the airline. The name chosen for the airline was "Virgin Blue." The truly wonderful thing is that all the planes are bright red. The whole thing is a wonderful "in" joke and shows how astute Richard is.

I am currently involved in a number of CodeCamp events. CodeCamp is a term that Microsoft evangelist Thom Robbins coined for a series of meetings he started in his area of the United States. We have adapted them via CodeCampOz and SQL Down Under Code Camp. Rather than hold these events in Sydney or Melbourne as might be expected, we have been holding them in Wagga Wagga. They have provided one form of periodic event that we have been very successful in rallying significant support for from around the country. For our CodeCampOz developer events in April each year, we have hundreds of attendees from around the country, and several now attend from overseas. For the first SQL Down Under event in October 2006, we were honored to have Itzik Ben-Gan (a SQL Server MVP from Tel-Aviv Israel) attend, along with a host of other excellent speakers and attendees.

Everyone involved in these events is doing so as a volunteer. They completely cover their own costs in attending. We love the idea of a weekend of technical content with a complete community focus. And I love the quirky nature of doing so in Wagga Wagga. The people of the town and Charles Sturt University who help by hosting us seem to love having us there too. Wagga Wagga might not exactly be in the middle of nowhere but they say you can see it from there.

Summary

This chapter emphasized that refreshments are not the most important aspect of user communities that meet face-to-face. They can, however, help provide a good atmosphere for networking amongst members and may persuade a member to attend rather than go hungry.

We discussed that technical people tend to like swag and that they can be driven to great lengths for comparatively small rewards if you can capture their imagination and competitive spirit.

Lastly, we discussed how periodic events can be used to reinvigorate volunteer efforts. These events can boost activity levels from existing volunteers and drive those who do not regularly help out to make a special effort.

Chapter 6

Don't Reinvent the Wheel

Organizing your community will be enough work without the need to constantly create new materials or ideas from scratch. Fortunately, this is neither necessary nor desirable. In this chapter we'll look at techniques to avoid it.

Learn from Other Groups

Over the years, I have spent quite a lot of time running training courses on various technologies. When I am working as a trainer, I sometimes get to attend classes run by other trainers. For trainers, attending a class has two purposes. One is that you might be there to learn the technical content of the material being covered. The other is that you might be there to see how to teach the class. These are very distinct issues. It's also one of the reasons why trainers don't tend to make very good students when mixed with other non-trainers in the same class. When you are learning the material with a view to teaching it yourself, you need to wonder about all the little odd questions that a student might ask you and it's easy to spend the entire class asking questions that the rest of the class would feel were inane and probably almost irrelevant. You do this because you know that every little thing that you wonder about during the class, will likely be a question you get asked one day by some future class attendee.

It is important that user group leaders and technical community leaders do the same. Make a point of attending other groups every time you have the opportunity. For example, if I am intending to visit another city, one of the first things I check is whether or not a user group meeting is occurring in that town on those days. But as well as taking in the technical content, spend most of your time watching the dynamics of the meetings:

- ▶ What works? And just as importantly, what doesn't?

- ▶ What does this group do differently to yours?

- ▶ How well do the members interact?

- ▶ How effective is the networking?

- ▶ What holds the members' attention?

- ▶ How is the meeting structured? Is it effective?

Allow time to talk to the leader of whichever groups you attend. Add them to your circle of contacts. Chances are, they'll be in your area sometime too and might perhaps do a presentation for you. Don't be ashamed to copy what works in another area. There is a good chance it may well work in your area. Ask the other leaders what they find difficult and how they currently deal with such issues.

Just as it is important for your group members to network with each other, it is important for people leading technical communities to network with each other.

Get Involved with Appropriate Community Organizations

To assist the networking of technical community leaders, a number of umbrella organizations have been springing up across a variety of technical disciplines. I will mention a few here as examples of the ones I have dealt with, but this list is far from exhaustive. It relates only to those groups relevant to the user communities I deal with.

INETA (www.ineta.org) is the International Dot Net Association. It is an umbrella group for developer user groups that are focused on Microsoft .NET technologies. It currently operates in five main regions that reflect the main regions of Microsoft activity: North America, Asia Pacific, Latin America, Europe, Middle-East, and Africa. It sources its funding from a number of sponsors but predominantly from Microsoft itself. It is an example of an organization that provides a collective way for a vendor (i.e., Microsoft) to deal with a large number of user groups without having to deal with each group individually.

INETA has a sister (or brother?) organization called Culminis (www.culminis.org) that performs the same role for user groups focused on Microsoft server technologies.

Each of these organizations has a concept of a speakers' bureau. It is centrally funded and sends high quality speakers out to individual user groups to make presentations. This allows local user groups to have occasional access to the rock-star style presenters of the technical world. So far, neither INETA nor Culminis tend to run significant independent conferences but they are involved in supporting smaller local activities, such as user group leadership summits and code camps, as well as participating in large conferences like TechEd and PDC.

PASS (www.sqlpass.org) is the Professional Association of SQL Server. Again, this is an umbrella group for user groups focused on Microsoft SQL Server. It is currently organized via a single management board that covers global activity. Each local member group is called a chapter. PASS differs from INETA and Culminis in that it manages significant technical conferences such as the annual PASS summit. This summit sees thousands of attendees mixing with industry luminaries and Microsoft product group members.

What these organizations provide though, is a mechanism for local user group leaders to maintain contact with each other through the organization. They also provide a vehicle for sharing ideas and innovations surrounding group and community activities.

While each organization will provide referrals to local groups from prospective members that have visited their Web sites, this is typically a small number of referrals. It is important to find other means to attract new members, rather than relying on referrals from umbrella organizations.

Ideally, user group leaders will form loose associations amongst themselves and use these for sharing ideas and asking each other questions. They might also use these loose associations to start to plan common events. In our region, we have found it effective to use e-mail lists for this purpose. For example, we have a .NET user group leader mailing list that covers Australia and New Zealand. On that list, we have most of the relevant user group leaders along with members of the Microsoft Platform Evangelism team for our region. This means that it is very easy for any user group leader to ask a question of all the other leaders or of our sponsor Microsoft.

If suitable umbrella organizations are not available in your technical area and you feel they would be useful, consider creating one. All the ones mentioned were created in this way in the first place.

Reuse Ideas Wherever Possible

User group leaders need to be endlessly keeping an eye out for ideas that have worked elsewhere. For most community and volunteer organizations, the origin of the good idea, while it should be acknowledged, isn't very important. You will also find that most people who come up with these good ideas will be more than happy to see them reused in other places, particularly if they receive attribution for them. Don't restrict yourself to ideas coming only from other technical communities. You will find it easy to adapt ideas from other types of user groups to use in your group.

Earlier, I mentioned our local code camps (www.codecampoz.com and www.sqldownunder. com). The idea for these originated with Microsoft's Thom Robbins in the New England area of the United States. When I contacted Thom about reusing the idea, he was only too pleased to see it happen. When I wanted to modify the logo and localize it, again I referred it to him as a courtesy and he was most pleased to see the outcome. In fact, he then did what he could to try to help promote our events. Most people with a volunteer inclination at heart are willing to assist you where they can.

In the involvement I had with INETA, I was privileged to see details of a number of community projects happening in areas such as India, Singapore, Brussels, and Latin America. The ideas are out there if you spend some time looking for them. Do not fall foul of the "not invented here" syndrome where people believe that ideas that originate elsewhere cannot be as good as the local ideas. Try to build yourself a network of like-minded community leaders from across the globe. Technology makes this easy today. You might also find you'll build some very good friendships from this too.

As a final example, I want to stress the need to also try to find new ideas that are just plain fun. At Microsoft TechEd (www.microsoft.com/events/teched) in 2005, members of the Microsoft Regional Director program (www.microsoftregionaldirectors.com) staged a set of talks called GrokTalks. (*Grok* is a common technical synonym for "understand"). While the idea of a number of technical talks at a technical conference is hardly surprising, the beauty was in the way these were delivered. Each regional director was invited to present a session taking no longer than ten minutes. They could speak on whatever they liked, to but it could not take longer than ten minutes. A special area was set up for holding these talks where a large screen and audio system was available. Again, there isn't anything special about this. The magic was in the marketing and fun level. The talks were described as being held at a secret location. Attendees had to find out where that was. A number of advertising images were created with a picture of a regional director with sun glasses on and looking almost in shock. The caption said "We've set our RD's on stun." I have not yet managed to find out who provided the real inspiration for this, but it certainly managed to capture quite a bit of enthusiasm. In addition, it provided some wonderful technical content, which was later made available for download (www.groktalk.net).

The great thing about this type of event is that it can be reworked and reused in different areas. While my local area doesn't have a pool of regional directors to draw on, we do have a local MVP (Microsoft Most Valuable Professional) community that might well be interested in trying something similar. The main lesson is to keep looking at what others are doing, acknowledge where the ideas came from if possible, adapt the ideas for your local conditions and try them.

Summary

In this chapter, we covered the importance of learning from other groups in your region and around the globe. An important role for a technical community leader is to be ever watchful of what is happening elsewhere and to try to adapt and reuse the ideas in the local area wherever possible.

Make a point of attending other groups every time you have the opportunity. Carefully watch the dynamics of their meetings to see what is working and what isn't. Learn from how their members interact and network. Note what holds the members' attention and what aspects of the structure of the meeting are most effective. Ask the other leaders what they find difficult and how they currently deal with such issues.

We also mentioned the value of umbrella organizations, such as INETA, PASS, and Culminis. Such organizations may offer a way for a vendor to deal with a large number of user groups collectively, rather than dealing with each group individually. They might also send high quality speakers out to individual user groups to make presentations, sponsor independent conferences, or support local activities. Umbrella organizations can help local user group leaders to maintain contact with each other.

Did you know?

It's likely that meeting attendees will retain only a small percentage of the technical content presented at the meeting but a very high percentage of the social content. Make sure they have time to network.

Chapter 7

Recruiting Members

A community is basically the sum of its members. One of the main tasks you need to pursue on a regular basis is recruiting new members for your group. A group without new members can quickly become stagnant. Fresh ideas are important.

Be Present at Events

Regardless of the technical specialty your community is based around and whether or not you meet face-to-face, it is highly likely that someone operates conferences and events that are relevant to you. It's important to have your community be represented at these events.

This doesn't mean that you personally need to attend each and every event. Hopefully, you will have built a bit of a team to help run things in your community. If you are a non-profit group and are very relevant to the event, I have found that most organizers will be happy to allow you to have some space. This might only be a corner of a room, but if you're lucky and there are actual booths, not all might be sold. Organizers also don't like to have empty booths at events. They may let you use an unoccupied one.

Even if you only have a corner of a room, it's important to have a visual presence. We found that if you can have a sign or image that can be seen from a distance, people will wander over to see what you are offering. In our case, we managed to get sponsorship from our local Microsoft team to print a banner on an X-frame. This photo is of the first banner we had made.

Figure 7.1: A Banner Featuring the Logo that Amanda Lee Designed for the Queensland msdn User's Group.

Some form of logo is important. You don't have to be a graphic artist to have one created. If you ask your members and have a small competition, you might well be surprised how many good options come your way. After I had received a number of good logo options, I passed them around the main volunteers in our community and had them vote for each. Because we were a Queensland-based group, the volunteers felt the logo we chose was ideal because it embodied beautiful beaches, tropical rainforest, wild flowers, a stark landscape, and ferocious burning sugar cane. Amanda Lee in the photo is the one who designed our logo. We were very proud of her efforts and have used the logo now in many places.

The X-frame in the photo also needs a mention. The beautiful thing about this style of device is that the banner rolls up and is stored in a tube alongside the X-frame when it is folded up. The entire banner can then be easily carried over your shoulder. It is also quite lightweight, even including the banner. Having a banner that is easy to move around is very important if you want to be able to take it to a lot of places.

At events, it might be acceptable to leave a small amount of information about the group near the display banner while sessions are on (if you plan to attend the sessions). However, I find it is a better idea to always have someone present at the stand during the entire event. If you have a small group of volunteers to work with and can set up a volunteer schedule, this is usually not an onerous task.

Community Organizations

I have never found that many new member registrations have come via any of the community organizations that we are members of. However, I feel it is absolutely worthwhile for your community to be a member of appropriate umbrella organizations. Very few people will directly visit the umbrella organization's Web site and then follow the link to your community, but I have found that people who are moving to new areas will often ask their existing local community leaders if they know what's available in the area they are moving to. Being a member of the umbrella organization makes it very likely that you will know that other community leader and the referral process is simple.

These comments do not apply to links from any sponsoring vendor though. In our case, links from the Microsoft Web site have been invaluable to us and have provided a steady stream of new members who otherwise might have taken a long time to find us.

E-mail

Many community leaders use their own e-mail signatures to show their affiliations and to provide a link to the user group. This can be surprisingly effective. I have added such links to my own e-mail signature periodically and included a link that I can easily track click-counts on. Each time I have enabled it, I have seen a steady flow of people clicking through to the group sites.

If you simply ask them, you may also find that many of your members will be willing to do the same. They will happily and often proudly show their affiliation to the group.

The same applies to postings you may make to other newsgroups, online forums, or e-mail lists. The key is to be seen where your prospective members are likely to be seen.

Ask Your Own Members

You will be surprised how many of your members will be willing to promote your community if they know you want them to do so. Periodically ask them to think about any other people they know who might benefit from taking part in your community. Find out which members are affiliated with or willing to visit your local colleges and universities to introduce them to your organization.

I don't believe in having large numbers of members who don't take part in the community. They aren't really members. I remember seeing a local user group recently that claimed to have over ten thousand members. Whenever I attend one of their meetings (they meet face-to-face), they seem to mostly have between twenty and forty people attending. It's then pointless to discuss having ten thousand members unless the membership is really used as some form of marketing vehicle and e-mail distribution list for some other reason, unrelated to the group's activity.

Ask Speakers to Help

If you have speakers coming from outside the existing group membership, consider enlisting their assistance in promoting their session. While doing so, they are very likely to uncover a whole new list of potential members for your group, particularly if they move in different areas than your existing members.

Often, speakers will be keen to promote their own activities and sessions within their workplaces, within the client bases, and within other technical communities in which they operate. Each of these could be helpful in locating new members for your community.

Keep Your Existing Members

The golden rule is to avoid losing your existing members. It is pointless to spend great efforts finding new members, getting them along to a meeting or to a community activity and then never seeing them again. In marketing, an adage is that the easiest customer to find is the one you already have. It is usually said about sales that it is ten times harder to find a new customer than to retain an existing customer.

Ideally, treat your existing members as long-term friends. Show genuine care and concern about their welfare. Take an interest in them. You will find it will be repaid many times over.

A good example of this is processing e-mails. I am a firm believer in handling all communication with members personally. I realize that this requires extra effort, but it builds more of a true community. I see many user groups where management of who's on the mailing list is done by an automated system. I believe they do this because they naively think it will save them time. Think about faceless systems you have dealt with in the past. Put yourself in the member's place. Would you rather deal with a community that gives you a URL for a Web site that will process their addition or removal from a notification list, or a community that has a leader or volunteer who says, "If you want to join or if you have any issue at all, just let me know and I'll fix it."

This really becomes important when people need to change details. Most automated sites work on the basis of using an e-mail address as an identifier. It is then usually very, very difficult for someone to work out how to change their e-mail address. Yet people need to do that all the time. I cannot stress how important it is for you to have an easy way for this to be dealt with by a human.

Also, consider for a moment why people change e-mail addresses. In a large percentage of cases involving technical communities, it will be because they have:

▶ a new job

▶ changed jobs

▶ lost their job

I always ask people about their address change in a personal but non-intrusive e-mail. Invariably I find they are just bursting to tell someone about something of significance that has happened in their lives. Don't let that moment be lost to an automated system. This a chance to build a true community of friends. Most of the time, you will have an opportunity to congratulate them.

However, if the news isn't good, you have the opportunity to express regret and to mention that you'll keep them in mind if you hear about anything happening that might be of interest to them. And if you do hear about something, make sure you let them know.

This is a key networking role you can perform as a community leader. It is very likely that from time to time you will hear of opportunities that might help members. Don't waste those opportunities. If you have a genuine interest in your members, you'll already know someone who might be able to take advantage of them. I have built some life-long friends from members of my communities and a number of them have initially come to my notice when their lives haven't been going well.

The last thing about e-mail relates to how you process bounced messages. If someone has gone to the trouble to join a notification list that you operate, chances are high that if you start to get bounced e-mails related to them, something of significance has changed. Invariably it means they have lost their job or changed jobs. Very likely, notifying you that their address has changed wasn't really high on their list of priorities at that time, because they are dealing with other things.

I find that it works well to collect bounced e-mails, sort and deal with them once you have more than one bounce for a particular address. I contact another member at the same organization that the e-mail was going to and ask them for help in sorting it out. Most times, this is all that is required. Periodically though (perhaps every year), I also include in my normal monthly mailing to members a list of members that we seem to have lost track of (i.e., just their names). I ask the other members if they can help shed some light on what has happened to them. Most other bounces get sorted out at this point. I find that if you are proactive on bounced e-mails, most can be sorted out quite easily and the member is pleased to be contacted again. This is another function that you do not want to leave to an automated system.

Another tactic which is often overlooked is to call a lost member on the telephone. It may seem that a person whose e-mail address has changed has also changed their telephone number, but that is not always the case. I recall how pleasantly surprised members have been when I have called them personally. This is truly a personal approach.

When you find a member who has moved away from your local area, send an e-mail to the user group leader in their new location. By referring one member to another user group, you reinforce your personal ties with both the member and the other user group leader.

Summary

In this chapter, we discussed techniques for finding new members for your technical community. Make the effort to have your community be represented at conferences and events that are relevant to you. If you are a non-profit group, organizers may allow you to have some space at the event, such as a booth or table. Be sure that your group has a strong visual presence, such as a sign or banner with an appropriate logo.

Other means of recruitment include involvement in community or umbrella organizations, e-mail links, and asking existing members and speakers for help.

We discussed a variety of ways to retain existing members. If you treat your existing members as long-term friends, show genuine concern about their welfare, and take an interest in them, you will be repaid many times over. We looked at several important ways that you can build up this relationship with members simply by the way you handle e-mail for your group.

Don't forget the key networking role you can perform as a community leader. If you hear of opportunities that might help members, pass them on.

*"Just swing it around in a crowded place.
You're bound to get a few new members."*

Did you know?

When you are consumed by your involvement in your community, it's very easy to assume that your group is widely known—because everyone you deal with knows about it. You'd be surprised to learn how few people actually know about your community. It's unlikely that you'll ever saturate the market.

Chapter 8

Content and Handouts

In this chapter, we will discuss the content for meetings. A key lesson will be to avoid "reinventing the wheel." In addition, we'll examine some tips for new speakers and discuss the usefulness of evaluations.

Reuse of Existing Materials

In a perfect world, each speaker will spend a great deal of time on research and will develop a new set of presentation materials from scratch. In that perfect world, time is always available for doing this and the resources required for creating the materials are always at hand.

In the real world, reuse of existing materials is essential. It is highly unlikely that the majority of presentations at your group are going to be completely original, unless your group presentations consist mainly of research findings by neighboring universities. It is far better to source appropriate materials that are already known to be interesting, to request permission to use them, and to spend what limited time is available on making sure the presentation of the materials is as good as possible. You will no doubt find that many members feel uneasy or reluctant to use materials produced by others. Help your member presenters get over that thought. Each will put their own personal touch on each presentation, regardless of where they have acquired the base materials. Giving credit to the original author will often build credibility for a speaker who uses existing high quality materials.

If your group is a member of an umbrella organization like INETA, PASS, or Culminis, it is very likely that such organizations can provide a repository for presentation materials from groups around the world. If the organization does not provide this, the time to discuss the creation of one with them is right now! Even if your group is not a member of such an organization (or when such an organization does not provide presentation materials as part of their charter), you should form a loose association with other group leaders in your country or region or even across the world.

Another good starting point is to ask to have yourself added to the mailing or notification lists for other groups with similar interests to your own, even if it is unlikely that you would ever be able to attend one of their meetings. You will then receive details of what the other groups are discussing. At the very least, this will provide you with an ongoing source of meeting topic ideas. If you notice a topic of interest, it would then be worth following up with the presenter to find out if you can get a copy of the materials for reuse in your own group. Most technical presenters seem to postpone finalizing their materials until the last minute, so it is likely that you would not get access to these materials until after the presentation has been made. You could then ask one of your group members to prepare the same materials for another presentation. This could be a very good option for a new speaker because it removes the worry about having suitable content and allows them to concentrate on the mechanics of the presentation.

For speakers who are keen on developing new materials, there are a number of good options that can make this easier. The technical organization or vendor that your group's meetings specifically target is likely to produce a wide variety of technical content that could be investigated to create a meeting topic. I will use Microsoft here as an example, because they are the company I am most closely associated with in the groups I organize and they provide a good selection of options for content generation.

Microsoft produces a large number of technical whitepapers. Often these whitepapers are produced to clarify some aspect of how to use their products. While they might not provide any detail that isn't available in the product documentation, that detail might not be very easy to discover in the original documentation. The aim of the whitepapers is to summarize disparate pieces of information or to explain how the product was intended to be used, as opposed to how it is able to be used. Best practices will often also be described. A document like this is a perfect starting point for a meeting topic. If the topic was important enough to produce a whitepaper on, it is likely to be of wide interest and not commonly understood. Most of these whitepapers will be copyrighted works, so ask the authors for permission if you intend to quote anything specific and provide a link for your audience to the original whitepaper. Occasionally, there will be reasons why this permission can't be given. If so, you need to respect that, but in my experience that is rarely the case.

Microsoft also produces a wide variety of technical webcasts. In these webcasts, experts on the topic (many of whom are often also seasoned presenters), provide an online interactive session. Most of the webcasts are available for offline downloading and viewing at a later time. Webcasts are perfect material for use directly as meeting content or for background research on a potential meeting topic. Again, my experience has been that if you contact the presenters and request permission to represent their materials, most are only too happy to do so. I have often had them send me additional material to that presented in the webcast. Make a point of directly crediting their work as the source of your content during your own presentation. Also ensure that you provide a link to their original presentation if it is still available.

Each year, Microsoft organizes a significant number of technical conferences around the world. Ideally, you should try to attend whatever conferences are relevant to your group. Each technical session in these conferences is a potential source of meeting content. Even when I have been unable to attend various conferences, Microsoft often makes available DVDs of most of the content. The same issues with permission and crediting existing work apply.

Even when you can't attend these conferences and shows, you can still benefit from their agendas. Get on the mailing lists of various conferences and you will receive their detailed lists of events with descriptions of each breakout session, the recommended audience, and the presenter (usually with their biographical information). This is a wealth of information for your meeting content. You will know what others are talking about, why it is important, and to whom it is important. You might even want to contact the speakers directly for more information or check out their Web sites, blogs, articles, and books.

Working from DVDs and watching webcasts are particularly powerful options for preparing new presenters. The new presenter can watch the session over and over again until the material covered is thoroughly understood and they can start to pick up subtleties in the material. If the original presentation was of high quality, they might also learn a lot about how to deliver the material.

Not everyone has time to sit and watch large numbers of technical presentations. My experience is that if I'm sitting at my computer, I am endlessly thinking of other things

I need to be doing on the system. I seem to get quite restless if I am watching these presentations. There are a number of things I have found to help with this.

I find I have more free time to listen to technical content while I am driving, travelling on public transport, or doing housework. In fact, I am now at the point where I would rather listen to a podcast than a radio station, every time. Although I host a technical podcast (SQL Down Under at `www.sqldownunder.com`), I listen to a wide variety of podcasts, not just technical ones. For example, I listen to:

► Mark Kermode's film reviews from the BBC

► Fly with Joe (a US airline pilot's show)

► Betty in the Sky with a Suitcase (a US flight attendant's show)

► The New Scientist podcast

► Mondays (a comedy show from Carl Franklin's PWOP Productions)

► A host of others

My iPod is now my favorite travelling companion when I am travelling alone. In the car, I use it with an FM transmitter add-on that lets me listen to it through my car's radio. Some cars now even have connectors for mp3 players. I mention this to emphasize the growing impact of podcast media and its potential to supplement a user group's offerings.

Rather than trying to watch the sessions from a technical conference on DVD, I find I have more success by copying the audio content from each session onto an audio CD and then listening to them. Most CD burning software seems to do a good job of extracting the audio from a video file if you simply drag the video file onto an audio CD that you are burning. Once I have extracted the audio, I often add it to the library for my iPod files. Even though I am not able to see the demonstrations from the conference sessions, I find I can follow the sessions well enough to know if they are of interest. If they really interest me, I then go back and watch the demonstrations on the DVDs at a later time.

Another tip I have picked up is to watch the sessions at higher than standard speed. In programs like Windows Media Player, there are normally buttons that allow you to increase the playback speed. The wonderful thing about this is that the audio is cleverly sampled rather than just sped up. This means that you can still understand the audio even when played back at twice normal speed, rather than having the presenter sound like some sort of cartoon character with a high voice. Listening to a large number of technical presentations provides a wealth of session ideas.

While I often make a significant number of presentations in any year, I also try to produce one or two significant presentations each year. For me, a significant presentation is one that takes around ten days of preparation work. Given the effort that goes into these presentations, it is important to gain good reuse from them. For example, for one presentation I created early last year, I ended up using it at my local group, at the Microsoft TechEd conferences in the United States, Australia and New Zealand, the PASS conference in Barcelona, the SQL Down Under Code Camp in Australia and the SQL Code Camp in New Zealand. I also ended up presenting it at a number of user groups around the country and recording it as a webcast for the Microsoft Developer Network (MSDN) in the United States. It also means that if I am travelling and I am called on to make a presentation at a local user group, I have a good selection of high quality materials to draw on. Reuse is wonderful payback for significant preparation effort.

Are Handouts Necessary?

At many presentations, attendees are given handouts with a copy of the presentation slides, usually printed about six per page. While there are conferences where this might be useful, in general the cost of doing this for most local user group meetings seems unjustified. My recommendation is that you let the speaker decide on this. If the speaker feels they are necessary, ask the speaker to provide them. Many will be happy to do so.

A better option is to make sure the materials are available to attendees after the meeting. If your community has a Web site (and it probably should), make a habit of chasing speakers for a copy of their presentation materials after the meeting and making them available via your Web site. Some speakers will not be keen to provide them (usually because they like to only make up-to-date versions available), but most will be happy for you to provide a link to the speaker's own Web site where the materials are hosted. You should contact the speakers after the meeting to thank them for presenting anyway, so simply add a request for a copy of the materials to your thank-you e-mail. A good repository of materials is useful for your members. It also means that prospective members can see a history of meetings and materials and realize that you operate a well-established group.

Evaluations

It is important to be able to provide feedback to speakers on how well their session was received. One way to do this is to have a formal evaluation system. If you are planning to do this, it needs to be painless for attendees. Ask questions which can be answered quickly with selection boxes or by grading on a scale. Only ask a maximum of 8-10 total questions. Make sure each question is clear and relates to one specific item that you wish to evaluate. Some questions will be the same for each presentation, such as general venue or time questions. Some questions will need to be specific to each presentation. Give your speaker an opportunity ahead of time to add a couple of questions specific to that presentation. Involving your speaker in the evaluation process is a great compliment—it makes the feedback relevant for that speaker and involves your members in a very intimate manner. Your members must know that they are also free to make any constructive comments in addition to the specific questions asked, and that all responses will be summarized and not tied specifically to individuals.

Print a copy of the evaluation form, leave one on every seat in the room and find a way to make sure they get completed. Have the evaluations completed immediately after the end of the presentation. Waiting any longer will dull the memory—you want fresh comments. The most common way to do this is to ask for them to be collected before the meeting ends and randomly draw one for some type of prize. You may need to check on local laws in relation to this though, as a number of jurisdictions have restrictions on raffles, competitions, and games of chance. There is usually some way around these laws that you can work with. For example, if a random draw is not permitted, a prize for a good question might be permitted. As a user group leader, it can be very useful to establish a pool of prizes to use for meetings.

If you do not use formal evaluation forms, it is still very important to gauge how sessions have been received. My personal preference is not to use forms, but to simply attend each and every meeting and spend some of the time observing how the audience is reacting. In addition, I make sure that before the meeting starts, I spend time discussing the previous meeting with group members. After each meeting, I spend further time discussing the current meeting with members. I often find that attendees will be much more specific (and far less guarded) in their comments when you are talking to them face to face than they will be on evaluation forms. A downside of using forms is that you only get feedback on the questions you ask. Forms tend to constrain the feedback process. Members completing forms at the end of a meeting tend to rush through and may not provide in-depth comments. If you spend time personally discussing meetings with group members, you will typically learn much more than you will from evaluation forms. A combination of forms and personal conversations is a good way to obtain overall evaluations.

Name Tags

A mistake I made for many years when running my groups was to assume that members of the group all knew each other fairly well. What tends to happen is that many of them recognize each other but do not know each others' names. One group I attended produced name tags for each member who had indicated that they would be attending the meeting. They also printed a member number as a barcode on the name tag, in a fairly unobtrusive way. They did this for a number of reasons. They used the left-over tags to gauge how many people said they were coming and then didn't arrive. They also asked each member to stick the name tag onto their evaluation form before they handed them in. This allowed them to follow up further on the member's comments if necessary and to know who had attended. In general, I find you get more credible feedback when you request it anonymously. You could also work out roughly who attended from the unclaimed name tags without needing to get the used ones back.

Nowadays, I find I do a lousy job of remembering people's names. I can recognize someone's face quite quickly and I can also remember a huge quantity of phone numbers but names just seem to elude me. I endlessly find myself feeling embarassed because I introduce two members to each other but can't recall their names. Constant repetition is the key to this. If members wear name tags during networking breaks, constant reinforcement of names seems to help greatly. Preprinted name tags are ok but my personal preference is to simply provide a quantity of large white adhesive labels and an oil pen and to ask members to write their name on a label when they arrive. I think it offers a more personal touch anyway.

You might consider a system where guests, visitors, and new members should be given name tags that stand out from the crowd with a different color or appearance. Draw attention to them in the meeting and make sure regular members welcome them.

Summary

In this chapter, we discussed techniques for locating and creating content for meetings. We emphasized the reuse of existing materials rather than "reinventing the wheel."

Umbrella groups sometimes offer a repository of presentation materials from groups around the world. Other user groups and their speakers may make their presentation materials available. Giving credit to the original author will often build credibility for a speaker who uses existing high quality materials. Technical whitepapers are great starting points for meeting topics. If the topic was important enough to produce a whitepaper on, it is likely to be of wide interest and not commonly understood. Webcasts are perfect material for use directly as meeting content or for background research on potential topics. Technical conferences—or even the agendas of these conferences—are another potential source of meeting content. Podcasts are an economical, timesaving, and convenient way to browse for meeting content. In all cases, be sure to give proper credit to your sources when necessary.

This chapter also evaluated the pros and cons of using preprinted handouts and evaluation forms. We concluded by discussing options regarding the use of name tags.

"Don't forget to take some handouts."

Part III

User Group Meetings and Conferences

RATIONAL PRESS

Chapter 9

Using Technology

At this point in the book, we hope it is clear that building a technical user community is not mostly about technology, it is about dealing with people. However, appropriate use of technology is still important. In this chapter, we discuss basic technology that can simplify your management of the community.

Registering and Contacting Members

Imagine yourself wanting to join a new community. There are two communities you can choose from. You send an e-mail to the leader of both to find out about joining. One leader sends back a link to the Web site for the community and tells you to follow a set of menus to find the place to register yourself. The other sends back a personal note that tells you a little about the community and offers to add you to the e-mail list for the group. He also tells you that if you need to change any of your details to just let him know and he'll fix them for you. I'd prefer to join the second group.

In this book I've been stressing the need for a personal touch when dealing with community members. Do not leave them to fend for themselves. Your members should matter enough to you that you are prepared to do simple administrative work for them. If you really do not have time to deal with those tasks, delegate them to a volunteer in your community. Make sure that joining your community is no more complex than sending you an e-mail. Next, make sure that any changes a member needs to make to their membership are also no more complex than sending you another e-mail. Tell the members that you will deal with any matters that need assistance and mean it. Make a point of never taking very long to respond to a member's e-mails either.

As your groups grow or you become aware that simply adding new members to your e-mail list has become burdensome to your volunteers, you might decide to use an automated approach to technology. While not as ideal, make sure it is one that doesn't remove the personal touch. Technology users may very well demand that your e-mail process is easy for them to modify on their own. The act of sending e-mails to join or change their address may be too much for some members. Don't make those tasks arduous for them. Make sure any automated e-mail service alerts you or one of your current members that there is a new person on your list or that someone has changed their profile data with your group. Follow up by sending them a personal welcome message (if they are new members) or a confirmation of profile changes (if they are existing members). They will know that a real person lies behind all that sharp technology and that you are personally interested in them.

I've regularly seen user groups that make users jump through hoops to deal with them. These groups lack much of what true communities offer. Dealing with issues that members raise is not a chore. It is a privilege.

Make sure that your Web site home page has an easy to find Contacts page link. I have seen too many user group sites that require a person to register just to find out the most basic information, including meeting location and how to contact the user group. Don't discourage people from contacting you—make it easy! Don't make it difficult to find your next meeting date or your location—it should be right there on your home page along with your Contacts link.

It is very important to protect the privacy of your members. Collect the bare minimum information that you need from them when they register with your community. For most of the communities I have been involved with, we normally ask for the following:

▶ Full name

▶ What they like to be called

▶ E-mail address

▶ Contact phone number (optional)

▶ Current employer (optional)

This list assumes that the group does not charge any form of membership fees. If the group does charge membership fees, it is likely that postal addresses will need to be kept along with details of any financial membership transactions.

I make it clear to members that I only collect a phone number for two reasons. One is that if they have registered to attend a meeting and something serious changes at the last minute, either a volunteer or I will try to call them. The other reason is that if I find their e-mail address consistently bouncing, I will try to call them to correct the situation. The current employer details are only used if their e-mail address consistently bounces and their contact phone number doesn't work. In that case, I try to locate any other member at that employer to help try to find them.

Never under any circumstances provide a member's contact details to another member. I often receive requests from members asking for details of how to get in touch with another member. In that case, my response is always that I will let the second member know that the first member is trying to get in touch with them. I then e-mail the second member and let them decide whether or not to contact the first member.

Similarly, do not allow your contact list to be used for any purpose other than that for which it was collected. If you have monthly meetings, try to avoid sending more than a single e-mail to each member each month. Most people already have more than enough spam hitting their mailboxes as it is. Do not add to the problem via your broadcasts. Unless your user group has sponsors, do not include anything that looks like advertising in the e-mails you send. Also, make your message consistent in format, subject line, and sender's e-mail address. This makes it easy for your members to recognize and filter your messages so that they do not end up in the junk mail folder or lost completely.

If you have a problem with people registering and then not arriving, consider sending no more than two e-mails per month, one to announce the meetings, one as a reminder on the day or the day before the meeting. A second message may be needed when your meeting is being held on a different date or time than usual or at a different location—anything that is out of the ordinary needs a reminder.

Given the small amount of information that you need to keep on members, you won't need any special technology to do this. For most groups without membership fees, a simple list in a spreadsheet would work fine. A small database would be better, but is not essential. If membership fees are charged, you are likely to need a small accounting package. There are many packages available to suit small associations. Ask other associations for their recommendations on this. Make sure to ask several before making a decision.

When sending details about upcoming meetings or events, my strong preference is that you individualize each e-mail. That means you would be sending out e-mails that begin "Dear Susan" or "Dear Terry" rather than ones that say "Dear Member." That is usually as far as you need to take this, but at least it is more personal. Most word processing programs such as Microsoft Word allow you to merge your letter with your mailing list held in a spreadsheet or a database. In recent years, anti-spam controls in programs like Microsoft Outlook try to prevent you from sending bulk e-mails by popping up a security dialog for each and every e-mail you send. If this is a problem for you, look around for programs or utilities that help work around it. I created a simple one for myself that looked for windows titled "Microsoft Outlook" and automatically clicked on the "Yes" button every time the dialog popped up. It was fairly crude but effective and I have also provided it to other user group leaders over the years. There are a number of such programs available. You should easily be able to work around these limitations.

In addition to individualizing each e-mail, my other strong preference is that you make it as easy as possible for members to register to attend your meetings or events. Unless a charge applies, members should need to do no more than to reply to your personalized e-mail to tell you that they will be attending.

Alternatively, include a one-click link to easily register, where member data is transferred automatically to the registration form and all your member needs to do is click to confirm. They should also be able to add comments and you should be able to easily access their comments. You should be able to easily and personally acknowledge their registration in this way. Again, I have seen user groups that make members take multiple steps to register for a meeting. What I have found over the years is that if you make it hard for people to register, they won't do so, but they often will still arrive at the event. If you get to that point, you have made your registration process pointless. The main reason most groups have a registration process for events is so they know who is coming, often to arrange catering.

Registration before meetings is not required in all cases. You may need to register for only special occasions when you know a larger or smaller than usual crowd will attend. When you begin registration for your regular meetings, it is best to continue the practice, so that your members won't question each month whether they are to register or not. Generally, registration for meetings is a good thing.

When a group member sends me an e-mail to say they will be coming to the meeting, I reply with a short e-mail thanking them for the prompt RSVP (if it was prompt) and mentioning in some way that I am looking forward to seeing them attend the meeting. While this might seem an unnecessary extra step, I have seen this produce great results. Before I started doing this, only about sixty percent of the members who would send an RSVP would end up arriving at the meeting. Once I started doing this, I noticed that figure suddenly climb to over ninety percent. I believe it is a direct result of them feeling that someone cares about whether or not they attend. It is an important personal touch.

I have mentioned this to other user group leaders and recall one telling me once that it was too much effort. He said, "It's ok for you if you're doing that for only seventy or eighty members." He then asked me, "How would you feel if you had to do it for one hundred and thirty members?" I told him I would be ecstatic to have that many people attending one of the routine meetings. Over twenty working days in a month, we are talking about less than ten e-mails a day. Each of these e-mails should take you a matter of seconds. If you are not prepared to send one hundred and thirty replies to members during a high attendance month, you need to reassess your interest in the group or your commitment to it. Alternately, you need to find a volunteer in your group who is willing to handle this.

In the groups I have been involved in, monthly meetings have been the norm. Each of the monthly communications I sent out contained the following:

- ▶ A thank you to the speaker from the last meeting.

- ▶ A thank you to the people who attended the last meeting.

- ▶ A genuine positive comment heard from a member who attended the last meeting (presuming you heard one).

- ▶ A short summary of the topic and presenters for the next meeting.

- ▶ Any important notices that members should be aware of.

- ▶ Details of the location and time of the next meeting, plus details of any special issues related to attendance. For example, one building we were meeting in had lifts that were locked at 6pm. Our meetings started at 6pm and members who were running late often could not get into the building. In the notice, we provided mobile phone contact details for people running late.

▶ A short biography of the presenters for the next meeting.

▶ A thank you to the sponsor (if any) for exactly what they provided (like refreshments and door prizes).

▶ More detailed information on each of the sessions in the upcoming meeting.

Another important tip is to make sure that any e-mails you send from your group are easy for e-mail client programs to categorize. For example, for our Queensland MSDN User Group, our e-mails would always have [QMSDNUG] at the start of the subject. For the Queensland SQL Server User Group, the e-mail subject lines would always start with [QSSUG]. Members will appreciate this.

If it is likely that a large number of your members will be using programs like Microsoft Outlook for managing their e-mail, you might also include a link to add your meeting directly to their calendar.

Hosting and Web Sites

While it isn't crucial that your Web site be stunning, you really need to have one. Your Web site will often be the first point of contact that prospective members will have with your group. It makes sense to ensure that they can find the key information they will be looking for. Unless fees are involved, I would recommend having all material on your Web site freely available for all to see. It is important that your site provides the following basic information:

▶ Full name of your group.

▶ Details of your group's aims, goals, or mission: why does your group exist?

▶ E-mail contact details. It may be preferable to slightly encode your e-mail address, such as leaving spaces in the address like travel @ codecampoz. com, so that Web sniffer programs don't immediately retrieve your addresses for spam senders.

▶ Date, time, and location of the next meeting.

▶ Details of speakers and topics for the next meeting.

▶ Details of how to RSVP for that meeting.

▶ Logos showing affiliations with umbrella organizations such as INETA, PASS or Culminis and links from those logos to the Web sites of the organizations.

Ideally, you would also provide the following:

▶ A repository of presentation materials from past events.

▶ Details of upcoming meetings (beyond the next one).

▶ Details of other user group meetings or related events, like code camps, seminars, and conferences.

▶ Phone contacts for your group (if you feel that is appropriate). Most user groups rely on the user group leader's home number. My U.S.-based colleagues do not encourage people to put their phone number on the Web site, but in personal messages they often include their mobile phone number so that speakers and sponsors can contact them in the case of emergency.

Getting started, you do not need to spend much money on a suitable Web site. Free community-built portal programs like Dot Net Nuke (www.dotnetnuke.com) allow you to very quickly set up a reasonable site.

Consider carefully how to host your Web site. Many organizations like INETA and Culminis have arrangements with companies that can provide free hosting. This can help to cut costs, but most hosting companies will offer free hosting only for legitimate user group purposes. If you are offered such hosting, do not abuse it by using it for anything even vaguely looking like commercial activity. If you did so, you could do harm to a large number of groups, not just to your own. Treat offers from companies that support groups like yours with great respect.

You will also need to decide on an appropriate domain name. If you are a completely non-profit organization, consider making that obvious by registering your name in the .org domain name space. If there are commercial aspects to your group, register it in the appropriate commercial name space. This will normally be .com but might also be a localized version, such as .com.au or .co.nz or .co.uk.

Try to make your Web site name reflect your user group name as it is spelled out, such as FultonCityDotNetUserGroup.org. Abbreviations may make sense to you and be short, but to most people they make no sense. If possible, it should be your exact user group name. Branding is important for name recognition—using a Web site name that is not the same as your user group name is just confusing.

Summary

This chapter discussed the appropriate use of technology in supporting your community, while keeping in mind the mantra that building a technical user community is not about technology, but about dealing with people.

Maintain a personal touch when dealing with community members. They should matter enough to you that you are prepared to do simple administrative work for them. Make sure that joining your community is no more complex than sending you an e-mail. Make it similarly easy to register for events. Personalize your e-mail communications whenever possible.

Protect the privacy of your members. Collect the minimum amount of information you need from them, and don't share it with anyone else without their permission.

Your community should have a Web site containing the basic information listed in this chapter. Give careful consideration to your hosting options and your domain name.

"Good thing we sent in our early registration packets."

Chapter 10

Recruiting Volunteers

This chapter covers a number of options for recruiting volunteers. First though, we'll discuss the importance of only recruiting people when you really have something worthwhile for them to do. We'll also discuss techniques for keeping them once you have found them.

Make it Worthwhile

In my experience, most people are essentially good natured at heart. Most will also rally to a cause when necessary. To make your cause one that they will want to help with, you need to somehow capture their imagination. Prospective volunteers need to see themselves doing something worthwhile and making a real difference.

A common mistake I see amongst user groups and user group organizations is to endlessly seek volunteers without a real plan and without specific tasks to be performed. For example, one umbrella organization that I was keen to help out endlessly advertises for volunteers, but they don't have any way to properly process people that offer to help. They had an e-mail address contact for volunteers to use. I e-mailed that address and was told by a prompt reply e-mail that they would contact me again soon to follow it up. No further contact was ever made, yet I constantly see them struggling to get projects happening with the two or three people working on them. The people doing the tasks seem too busy doing the work to help integrate anyone who wants to help them out.

This example shows the importance of personnel and task management. This doesn't just apply to volunteer organizations. It's a general problem with delegation that occurs throughout workplaces. It reminds me of a story that my previous business partner Peter Dean used to tell. He was involved in marketing a system product that we produced. He said it reminded him of a battlefield general who was too busy fighting a battle with bows and arrows to spend time listening to what the tank salesperson was trying to tell to him.

People will be willing to help you, but you need to do the following:

▶ Make it clear to them what the ultimate goal is.

▶ Make it clear to them how they can help.

▶ Make it clear to them how their contribution will take you towards that goal.

I believe the first step is to gain a shared vision. Whatever your plan is, volunteers need to know where you intended to end up. They don't want activity for the sake of activity, and they certainly don't want to undertake administration tasks for the sake of administrative outcomes. You need to somehow plant a picture in their minds of exactly where you are headed, how that ultimate goal would look, and how wonderful it would be to get there.

At this early stage, you and your volunteer will also determine if the tasks at hand are those that the volunteer wants to do, has the ability to do, and has the time and resources to do. This is a time of discovery. Don't assume that once a volunteer has come forward that they are the best person to complete the tasks. If the person needs assistance, get it for them if you can. If the person is not correct for the tasks, make sure to find different tasks for them.

Next, you need to make it clear exactly what you want them to do. Don't expect them to just jump in and start making decisions if they don't feel they have the authority to do so. If you do let them start making decisions, be prepared to back those decisions and not criticize them. Most volunteers in technical communities will be very capable people in their own right and quite capable of making a variety of decisions. Make sure you are giving them tasks that allow them to do this. Ideally, try to find a task for each volunteer that has a distinct outcome, so that they can feel some sense of ownership of that outcome. This can make them feel that it's all worthwhile.

Finally, you need to make it very clear how their contribution—no matter how small—will help achieve the ultimate goal that you both share. The critical thing is to never waste their time. I often see this happen. When groups are not sufficiently organized, projects are often ill-defined. Volunteers can be assigned to tasks that end up at dead-ends or with their work being disposed of. This will be soul-destroying for the volunteer. You will lose their interest and may even lose them from the community. It will certainly be much harder to ever gain their interest in any of your projects again.

It would be far better to have never enlisted a volunteer in the first place than to have them feel that their time and effort has been wasted. If your project really is disorganized, get the volunteer to help organize it, rather than assigning them to a task that has the potential to lead nowhere. If after all your best efforts, a task that a volunteer has been undertaking needs to be terminated, it is very important that you discuss the situation with the volunteer, show them the alternatives for moving forward and enlist their opinions on how to proceed. While they won't be happy at disposing of any of their efforts, they will feel much better about it if they were part of the decision-making process that was involved. If this has to happen, try to make it a very, very rare outcome.

Volunteer contracts can be formal or quite informal. I like the informal ones best. They can be written and agreed to by both you and your volunteer by e-mail after you have had a personal conversation. Make the agreement state in clear terms what they are to do, following the guidelines above.

Finding Volunteers

I mentioned in an earlier chapter that a session I attended at the INETA worldwide conference made a key point about finding volunteers. The main thing you need to do is to actually ask people to help. I regularly hear people talking about how hard some task was or about something worthwhile that didn't get achieved. In the next breath, I hear someone else say to them, "I wish you'd have asked me. I would have really liked to have helped with that."

I have never found it difficult to enlist the help of volunteers. The first step is to get to a point where the prospective volunteer shares your vision of the results that will be achieved. You need that little light bulb to go off in their heads that says, "That would be just awesome" and then another one that says, "I could play a key part in making that happen."

Another area of great concern is the never-ending volunteer commitment request. When faced with a large number of tasks to perform, some very willing people will decide not to volunteer because the picture being painted is one that seems to go on forever. It is much better to segment large tasks into smaller tasks. They are much easier to manage and will get commitments from some members who would not or could not commit to a longer time frame. Be specific about the number of hours you expect a task to take and how often it needs to be done. You will be amazed at the number of people who will contribute in this manner.

Once that shared vision is implanted, the next step is to ask for a volunteer for a specific task. It is very important that the task is specific. A common mistake I see is for people to ask very generally for help. For example, compare these two requests:

1. Our user group is always in need of helpers. If you'd like to help, please contact us at xxxxx@somegroup.org.

2. We're trying to organize our annual conference. We need a capable person who's willing to coordinate requests from members for travel and carpooling assistance. We need this person to generate a frequently asked questions section for our Web page that covers how to get to and from the conference. Research on available airline, bus, and train schedules will help a lot in creating this. We also need the person to process e-mails from members who want to share vehicle costs when driving to and from the conference. This involves matching people up for travel purposes. Lots of members usually ask for help with this—your volunteer efforts can make a real difference to the overall success of the conference.

Which would you be more likely to want to help with? I'd take the second request every time. It fills several criteria for a successful outcome. It shows what we're trying to achieve. It clearly explains what is needed from the volunteer and it makes sure the prospective volunteer knows that doing this role well will have a strong positive outcome on the final goal.

The first request might be okay for general expressions of interest, but if you receive a reply to it, it would be important to promptly let the prospective volunteer know the following:

► Assistance requests pop up from time to time.

► Their offer to assist is really appreciated.

► They will be contacted whenever an assistance request appears.

When a specific task arises that you need help with, make sure you send it to each and every person who has replied to one of these general requests. Don't leave them dangling and wondering if they will ever be contacted again. Even if you don't take up their offer immediately, they won't feel like they're out of the loop if they see e-mails with assistance requests, other e-mails confirming that someone has taken on a task, and thank you e-mails to all those who offered to help. Correspond with them regularly, even when you don't have a specific task for them to perform.

If someone volunteers in a general way, make sure to periodically involve them in a task. If you have too many volunteers and too few tasks, find something worthwhile for them to do. I don't mean a throw-away task. Look long and hard at your community and think about things you'd like to tackle, if you only had time to do it. Then, if you don't have time to organize them, find a volunteer capable of organizing and let them do so. And tell yourself that in future, "I won't ask for volunteers again unless I already have something worthwhile for them to do."

Where to find volunteers is often a pretty easy question to answer. For most technical communities, the existing members already share your vision for the community to at least some degree, so they would be a great starting point. You can ask for volunteers when you have a presence at conventions or conferences, but I think this is a better forum to look for prospective members than for prospective volunteers. A person should feel committed to your community before you ask them to volunteer to help out.

Keeping Volunteers

Every now and then, I see surveys of employees that ask what makes them stay with their current employers. Most people assume that a high salary is a key indicator. In some areas it might be, but for technical people it often rates well down the list. Technical people tend to list other items, such as:

▶ Working on interesting projects

▶ Recognition

▶ Working with bleeding-edge technology

▶ Working with clever people

▶ Keeping up-to-date personally

▶ Constantly being challenged

When you are working with volunteers who are technical people, this is a very positive thing, because you normally don't have any salary to offer them! However, all the other aspects that made it to that list are things you can provide to volunteers at no cost.

The one I want to make special mention of is recognition. I mentioned in the last section that volunteers like to work on tasks that they can make their own. Part of this is driven by a need for recognition. My experience is that volunteers will expend enormous efforts on tasks that can be clearly recognized as being associated with them. They want to feel that they have accomplished something that matters, but they also want it to be recognized that they were the ones that accomplished it.

A common mistake that employers make is to not acknowledge their employees' good work. I spent many years working for Hewlett-Packard in Australia. Several of the managers seemed to understand this concept well. We often worked exceedingly long hours and I had a travel schedule that was almost ridiculous. But I clearly remember each and every time that a manager did something on the spur of the moment, such as sending me a bottle of port with a note thanking me for some special effort. The port didn't cost much, but it was worth far more because it was special and out of the ordinary.

In the late 1970s, I was developing systems at a professional photo laboratory. Each Christmas time, the manager would take the staff and their wives, husbands, or partners away for the weekend to a mountain lodge or to a beach resort at the Gold Coast. As a wonderful extra nicety, his mother (the managing director) would present each staff member with a Christmas gift. Being young and naïve, I recall asking him about whether he thought the cost was justified. He just looked at me wisely and explained it like this: "I work them all very, very hard all year long. I get back from them many, many times the value of what it costs me for that one weekend each year. Yet all year long, when talking to friends and family, they don't talk about the effort they put in; they talk about the Christmas weekend away."

The irony of all this is that often in exit interviews, staff who are leaving companies say they didn't ever feel like they were doing a good job. Employers then invariably say, "But you were doing a great job." And the answer usually is, "You never told me that before now."

Make a point of recognizing the efforts of your volunteers, particularly in public forums. Post their names on your Web site (if they are okay with that), make a small note in your monthly e-mail message, and above all, recognize them personally during your meeting. Take a moment to call them on the phone and follow up with an e-mail message. When their time and efforts intruded on their personal or family time, contact their friends and family to thank them, but make sure to ask your volunteer for permission first. When their company was involved in their volunteer efforts, make sure to recognize the company contributions as well. You can't thank people enough. Be sincere and make your thanks meaningful. They will notice it and their sense of pride in having accomplished something worthwhile that has been recognized will drive them to do even more next time.

Summary

In this chapter, we discussed a number of options for helping you to recruit volunteers. A key aspect is simply making sure you ask them, but more importantly, make it clear to them what they will be doing and how it is important to achieving an ultimate goal. Make sure they share your vision for that goal. We also discussed how critical recognition is in retaining volunteers and getting even more from them.

Did you know?

Being flexible with how your volunteers perform a task greatly increases their perception of their role. While you might do a task differently yourself, make sure you give your volunteers a chance to act as individuals.

Chapter 11

Conducting Meetings

While there are no hard and fast rules for how meetings should be conducted, in this chapter we will look at how they are commonly structured. We will also look at pitfalls to avoid.

Multiple Topics or Just One?

By this stage in the book, it should be pretty clear that my preference is for each meeting to cover more than one topic. This greatly increases the chance that every member attending the meeting will take away something worthwhile. My other strong preference is that the two presentations in the meeting have different levels of technical complexity and deal with different subjects. Most experienced members will happily tolerate a topic that is a review of basic material. In fact, they will usually still learn something from it and may help contribute to any discussion surrounding the topic. They will often "fill in the blanks" from their own experiences. Newer members are then also less likely to feel like the entire meeting was over their heads and never return.

The two topics for the meeting don't even need to have any relationship to each other, but there's no rule that says they can't. I am normally happy to just run with whatever appropriate sessions come along and are scheduled. However, having two different topics provides an opportunity to attract members who may have an interest in one topic but not both. Having two different topics provides two reasons to attend.

It is important that speakers on any complex topic have adequate time to cover them at the required level. In general, I find that about half an hour on an introductory topic and about an hour on a complex topic works quite well. I have seen other user groups that have meetings that run for three or more hours, but I am not a fan of this at all. Those groups tend to have a smaller but loyal following. I don't want a meeting to feel arduous in any way. There shouldn't be any heroics involved in making it to the end of a meeting.

This is, of course, up to you and your membership. Some user groups have gotten along quite well by filling all available time with various activities that tend to make the meetings long. In my experience, the number of presentations and other activities can go on all night if the members want. To drone on for hours on one subject by one speaker is not what we are talking about here—it's the excitement of wanting to continue even in the face of the ticking clock. You can provide a variety of activities but still avoid a long meeting if you provide an agenda. Members can come and go for those portions of the meeting that are important for them, although for night-time meetings that would be less appropriate.

Respect Members' Time

While I am a fairly laid-back sort of person and try to make any meeting appear fairly casual and friendly, there is one area where I never compromise. I try to make sure that all meetings start on time and that the speakers keep fairly close to their allocated times. This is all about respect.

I learned this while coaching youth baseball, softball, and soccer teams. I saw many teams over the years that held practice sessions that did not start on time and then regularly ran over the finishing time. While this may have suited a few of the parents who were running late, it was greatly disrespectful to those who didn't. It is very important to do the right thing by those who do the right thing by you. I found that parents greatly appreciated practice sessions that started on time and, just as importantly, finished on time. People have lives that are very complex and they are already fitting your activity into that time. Don't make them regret doing so.

I found exactly the same thing when my children started their first jobs. In Australia, fifteen and sixteen year olds can work but they can't drive cars. That means that parents usually need to take them to work and pick them up, unless they are in the fortunate position of living close to where they work. Invariably, companies such as the fast food chains require their staff to arrive for work well before their allocated start time. However, they also tend to be lousy about letting their staff leave when their shift is meant to finish. Because they are often working at night, parents feel compelled to come to collect their children from work for safety reasons. What I usually found was that I ended up sitting in the car park waiting for my daughter for up to an hour after her shift was to have ended.

This was greatly disrespectful of my time. I didn't work for the company, yet they were wasting significant amounts of my time each week. Make a point of always respecting the time of your members.

In a similar vein, when someone does the wrong thing, don't penalize someone who's doing the right thing. Don't limit the time for a punctual speaker just because another speaker is running over the allocated time. If you have a half-hour introductory level topic followed by an hour of a more complex topic and you allow the first speaker to take 45 minutes or an hour, you are being very unfair to the speaker who follows. He will then feel compelled to fit a complex topic into a shorter time. Do not underestimate how aggrieved people can be if they feel they are doing the right thing and they are being penalized for someone else's error.

Make every effort to truncate the first speaker at or around the allocated time. Suggest that further discussion could be taken offline after the meeting. Alternately, suggest getting the same speaker back to continue the discussion at another meeting. If a topic runs too long and the interest is high, perhaps this topic should have been a major meeting topic rather than a minor one. Only do that if the interest level really is high. Don't do it if you simply have a speaker who is not organized enough to fit their presentation into the allocated time.

New presenters will often fall foul of this because they will prepare way too much material. Chapter 12 details some tips and techniques for helping new presenters to avoid these problems.

Limit the amount of time you spend on user group administrative issues. It is desirable to completely divorce regular user group meetings from those that are specific to administering the user group itself, which should take place on a different day altogether. Sometimes it will be unavoidable, but in your regular meetings, spend as little time as you possibly can discussing the issues of running your user group.

While we are referring to speakers, be sure that you as a leader are also not guilty of starting late, running long, or generally not abiding by your planned agenda. When you have refreshments, make them available during the half hour prior to the start of the meeting, so your precious speaker time is not compromised by members feeding themselves. To assist in that, place the food in an outer room if possible, and close the food down when your actual meeting time starts. Also, make sure there is enough food for almost all members who plan to attend—those who arrive early get to eat; others may not find anything left. That's not cruel. What is cruel to your fellow members and to the speaker is people coming in late and eating during a presentation.

Meeting Content Ideas

While the format of your meetings needs to reflect what works for your members, you might want to choose from some of the following ideas.

New Member Introductions

Taking a few minutes to introduce new members is usually a good idea. I normally get people to share who they are and something about their job role. This allows other members to acknowledge them and will often prompt existing members to make a point of saying hello to them later, particularly if their workplace or job role is of interest. Don't expect the newcomers to say too much, because they will usually be a bit timid at first. This is also a great time to ask the new attendees how they found out about your group. Keep track of what is actually bringing in new members.

Introductory Topics

These are a great option for making sure all members can get something out of each meeting. Even experienced members will usually take something away from these. They also make a good starting point for new presenters. Don't make them too long though, unless the entire meeting is devoted to a topic that very few people in the group know about. For example, an Introduction to Data Mining might help a group of developers, yet very few might know anything much about it.

Advanced Topics

This should be the main content of each meeting. If your group is to have a reputation for high quality, there should be a constant stream of advanced topics, presented by experienced presenters. While groups can flounder when all the topics are advanced, they will also flounder if all the topics are introductory.

You will need to judge your membership and their tolerance for introductory and advanced topics. Remember, even advanced topics are introductory to those who have never experienced them before, and even to beginners, some topics are advanced. The point is that more often than not, offer something for everyone in various flavors and levels, then get feedback.

Member Tips and Tricks

One thing I like about Adam Cogan's user group is that he has a session early in the night where members share any new tips and tricks that they have found during the month. Adam lets them describe these quite patiently and takes the time to ensure he understands what is being suggested. Other members seem to really appreciate this. This session must be kept to a specific time limit though. In any discussion-oriented session, time can easily get away from you, and the main sessions of the meeting can be impaired.

News, Notices, and Upcoming Important Events

Most months, I found I had a series of upcoming meetings, events, and notices to let members know about. If an event is coming up in three months, make sure you mention it at every meeting from the time you find out about it until it occurs. Even though you might feel you have mentioned it before, you will often have a somewhat different group of people in the room and they may not have heard it mentioned before. If you have any special offers from vendors, display them on your Web site or mention them briefly in your notification e-mails. Mentioning them at meetings will start to turn the meeting into a sales pitch and may well disappoint many users. Unless the vendor is offering something extra special for members of the group that isn't available to the general public, I wouldn't even list it on the site. You are not there to be the marketing arm for vendors.

Reports from Recent Events

If significant events have taken place since the last meeting, it may be worthwhile to ask a member who attended them to spend a few minutes reporting on the event. This type of session works best if they have photos from the event to share and can mention a few specific takeaways that they valued.

Surveys

Periodically, you might wish to survey your members to gauge their level of interest in proposed meeting topics. In general, this is best done in face-to-face discussions. However, surveys are useful to gauge interest in something out of the ordinary, such as a proposed hands-on workshop day. Unless you're asking pretty simple yes/no style questions, I wouldn't spend too much valuable meeting time on surveys.

Group Problem-Solving Sessions

Some groups value having sessions in which members can describe their intractable problems to see if other members can help. While group discussions may end up providing the answer to a problem, often they end up producing alternate approaches that might be taken. The size of your meetings will determine if this style of session would work for you or not. The larger the meeting, the less likely this is to be workable when trying to avoid boring too many members. You may be able to improve the quality of these sessions by asking members to submit their questions in advance, perhaps while they are registering their attendance at the meeting. You could then vet the questions and make sure that those that are discussed are likely to have wide interest or be particularly challenging. For questions that are routine, you might be able to ask an experienced member to help the person solve the problem.

Group Brainstorming Sessions

These are similar to group problem-solving sessions, but again, they really work best when the meeting has a small number of participants. Alternately, these are better handled as special one-off small group sessions, separate from the main meeting.

Open Group Discussions

These really get your group talking. Here you are usually opening up a discussion on a non-technical but related topic. These are wonderful sessions for your user group because they give your members a rare chance to interact on topics that are important but not often given sufficient time. Your user group members are a great source of these topics. These should be announced ahead of the meeting, perhaps in your newsletter or meeting reminder e-mail so that members can prepare thoughts and questions.

Decide on a title that describes the topic and be unprejudiced. Construct two sets of descriptions—one for each of two sides of the discussion—and announce them in advance. Try omitting questions and instead include statements. Remember to take a high level view—defining terms can be trickier than you think! Both of the arguments need to engage the audience with statements for each side of the discussion. Open the discussion to the floor with a reading of the descriptions and any provocative statements needed to get the juices flowing. You will need two unbiased moderators to limit the individual statements. Here are some examples:

▶ Business Needs vs. User Wants—Is there a Disconnect?

▶ Web vs. Windows Applications – What's your Opinion?

Keep Control of Discussions

One of your main tasks as a community leader will be to keep meetings under control. While free-ranging discussions can be a wonderful thing at your meetings, there are a number of areas you need to watch out for.

First, don't let any individual dominate discussions. You will find individuals who seem to like the sound of their own voice. At times, this will be because they are trying to make a big show of their knowledge on the topic. While there is a chance that they might impress whoever they are trying to impress, the more likely outcome is that they will bore everyone else senselessly. A dominant person will also tend to stifle the very discussions you are trying to encourage. Others will be too timid to offer their own opinions, even though they may well be more valuable.

Second, keep the discussion on track. Anyone who has participated in e-mail threads has had the experience where they wonder, "How did we end up discussing nuclear fusion reactors in a thread that was about the required specifications for product XXX ?" Exactly the same thing can happen in free discussion periods. You need to watch carefully to see if the discussion is staying on track. Even if half the room wants to take the discussion onto some unrelated topic, the other half will not appreciate you letting it do so. As soon as you sense this is going to happen, be prepared to intervene and move the discussion offline.

Third, watch for any commercial issues, privacy issues, or any material that could offend a member or land someone in hot water. Never allow any form of discussion that would be at all libelous, and quickly curtail anyone making sexist, morally offensive, or nasty remarks. If someone does this, do not try to argue with them (much as you might want to), because that will only make things worse. I learned many years ago from my time as a baseball umpire that you can't argue with someone who won't argue back. If ever anyone came out to argue a point in a game, I would stand there and listen intently but wouldn't comment. No matter how upset they are, they will eventually stop if you don't argue back. Then I'd just make a comment like, "OK, you've had your say; I've noted it. Let's get on with the game." They'd usually look a bit dumbstruck and just walk away. No matter how bad a comment or discussion is, it is best to immediately divert the discussion, not enter into it. Say something simple like, "Sorry, but that's inappropriate for this meeting, let's get back to XXX." Hopefully, you won't have to deal with anything like that, but you need to be prepared.

While I have only once had to deal with a situation like that, I have had to deal with speakers who decide to tell jokes or show pictures that are clearly inappropriate. Even if a large number of people in the room find it amusing, you could well lose a few forever. That's not worth allowing. Signal to the speaker that it is inappropriate and counsel them on it later.

Summary

In this chapter, we discussed different types of sessions that you might use in a face-to-face meeting. While there are no hard and fast rules for how meetings should be conducted, we have considered what is likely to be a good mix. Each meeting should cover more than one topic. This greatly increases the chance that every member gets something worthwhile from it. Also, the two presentations in the meeting should have different levels of technical complexity and deal with different subjects. Be sure the speakers have adequate time to cover the topics at the required level.

Respect your members' time. Keep the meeting on track, on time, and on topic. Don't limit the time for a punctual speaker just because another speaker is running over the allocated time. Sharply limit the amount of time you spend on user group administrative issues, or deal with such matters in a separate meeting.

We discussed meeting content ideas: introductions, introductory and advanced topics, tips and tricks, news and upcoming events, event reports, surveys, problem-solving and brainstorming sessions, and open group discussions.

No matter which content ideas you choose, be sure to maintain control of the discussion. We looked at techniques for avoiding potential arguments and nasty situations, although we hope that such things will be very rare.

Chapter 12

Tips for Presenters

In this chapter, we will cover a number of tips and techniques used by experienced presenters, and some that are meant specifically for new presenters.

Preparing New Presenters

A common mistake for new speakers is to prepare way too much material for their presentations. If you have less experienced speakers presenting introductory-level topics at the beginning of a meeting, you are likely to have them run way over their allocated time. New presenters are often very nervous. They compensate for their lack of confidence in the quality of their material by providing way too much of it. I try to provide some level of coaching to new presenters, particularly if they ask for help. I often see new presenters with thirty or forty slides prepared for a half hour session. At first they think I'm joking when I suggest to them that for a half hour session, they should probably have way, way less than that.

Fellow Microsoft Regional Director Adam Cogan tells me that he asks new presenters at his user group to come along and make their presentation to him prior to their appearance at the meeting. This could be earlier in the day or on a prior day. I admire Adam's efforts in this regard in trying to keep the quality of presentations at his group high. Even if you don't have time to do this, it is important to ask new presenters to run through the material on their own, to roughly work out the timing of their session. By the time you introduce yourself and the topic and summarize what you've covered at the end, you don't have a huge amount of time to cover significant detail in a half-hour session. It is important that it is delivered sharply and very much to the point. This is particularly the case for introductory material that the audience will absorb quite quickly.

Years ago, I started presenting at Microsoft MSDN events around the country. The first stop on those tours was usually a lunch time "brown bag" session held in Microsoft's offices where any of their staff who were interested in the topic would come along to hear it. The internal Microsoft person sponsoring the event would also attend. This allowed them to make sure the presentation was of suitable quality. It also allowed them to make sure you weren't about to make any incorrect promises or statements, given you were going to be representing them around the country. I found the brown bag session to be quite valuable. I received some great technical feedback from their staff that I was then able to incorporate into the sessions I ended up delivering on the trip.

General Presentation Tips

I regularly see tips and tricks for presenters that I know were not written by experienced presenters. I especially love the nonsensical ones that tell nervous people to do things like "imagine the audience in their underwear." The list provided here is not exhaustive, but these are the tips that I have found most useful.

Find an Appropriate Topic

This might seem obvious but unless you pick a topic that people are interested in, it won't matter how well or how poorly you present; they won't like it. Chapter 8 presented some ideas on finding topical content.

Have a Structured Session

Each session needs to have structure. You need to open with a clear message about what you are going to cover and why it is important for the audience, not just why it is important to you. You need to close with a clear summary of what has been covered, details of any other resources attendees might use, and a call to action where that is appropriate (i.e., tell them what they should look to do next). In the body of the session, you need to have further structure. In most sessions that are around 60 to 90 minutes overall, I like to have about three main topics in the body of the session. For each, I like to introduce the topic, cover the material, and then demonstrate anything that it is possible to demonstrate in the allowed time frame.

There is an old statement that is so true—tell them what you are going to tell them, tell them, and tell them what you told them. The point here is to make sure you get across the most important point(s). Repetition is fine when it assists your audience in getting it.

Get the Timing Right and Be Punctual

Don't be rude to other presenters or to the organizers. Be prepared to start on time and make sure you have timed your session so that you will be off on time. Until you have quite a bit of experience, it will take some practice to get the overall amount of content right to ensure correct timing. Many presenters like to see a count-down clock, etc. on their screen to let them know where they are on the timeline. A clock tends to insert some form of urgency into my presentation and voice. I don't ever want the presentation to sound rushed. I would rather have some optional material that I could discuss if I have time and leave it out if I am short on time.

Being prepared to start on time means *ready to start*, not ready to walk to the front of the room and start getting ready. If you are using a computer and it takes a while to start up, make sure it has started well before it is needed. Test any screen projection equipment to make sure it works, well before it is needed. Again, check any audio-visual equipment, microphones, computer audio, or video systems well before they are needed. You don't want to start your session looking rushed or flustered. You want to look relaxed and confident. For some presenters, that might also mean making sure you have visited the bathroom before starting too.

Make sure to work out these logistics well before your time to start. Even the simplest of items may not work the way you assumed. Chris Wallace told me of one presenter who was totally taken by surprise when the lights in the room would not go off, due to some ordinary emergency lighting that was required to stay on. Don't take anything for granted. Discuss your processes with a person familiar with the venue and the equipment you will be using. User group leaders should be familiar with their regular venue characteristics, and go over everything ahead of time, especially anything out of the ordinary.

By the way, check the battery levels on any wireless microphones. This is part of your equipment check and pre-meeting preparation.

To Use PowerPoint Slides or Not?

There is a myth that technical presentations that don't use any slides are better than the ones that do. I have seen appalling presentations from people using no slides at all where even though the presenter is technically capable, the session has no structure that the audience can see and the presenter just seems to fumble along. Slides can also help you avoid forgetting key points. I often hear presenters without slides endlessly saying "Oh and another thing I should have mentioned…"

I believe that presenting the content that the audience wants to know about in an entertaining way is far more important than whether or not you use slides. Directly against all assumed knowledge, the best scores I have ever received for a Microsoft TechEd presentation were for a session I did with 100% slides. I didn't do a single demo. I truly didn't think that was possible but I risked it and it worked very well. What I did do was provide a large amount of directly relevant content. I spent over two weeks reading every single post in a newsgroup forum on the topic. I read over 10,000 posts. I made sure the session covered every single worthwhile question that had been raised in that forum. I presumed that if lots of people wanted to know about it, it would make a good session. It did.

In general though, I use a mix of slides and demonstrations.

Use Appropriate Fonts

A very common error is presenting using fonts that just can't be read clearly at the back of the room. I find that for the programming sessions I deliver, I use 14 point or even 16 point fonts. Being able to read what's on the screen is more important than having to occasionally scroll the screen to show things off to the side.

Another common mistake is to use highlighting that makes the text harder to read. In most applications, selected text is shown by default with dark blue or black backgrounds. When highlighting sections of programming code or words in documents, that is not suitable. You need something that is more like a highlighter pen that has good contrast. I routinely use a yellow background with black text for my selected text.

While on the topic of fonts, don't forget to update them on all the places that might be displayed: results panes, Internet Explorer windows, notepad, Microsoft Word documents, etc. If managing all these is just too much work, a good tip I saw from Scott Hanselman is to set up another logon account on your computer, set up specifically for doing presentations. As with most things, consistency is the key.

Demos Must Work

Again, this seems bleedingly obvious but I have lost count of the number of sessions where technical demonstrations just didn't work. There are very, very few valid excuses for this. Your demos must work.

If the unthinkable happens and your demos do not work, you must accommodate that possibility. Don't try to salvage something that is not going to work. Move on. Above all, do not attempt to fix it on the spot if it appears to be more than something very simple. It is not worth it—you will lose your audience and the remainder of your presentation will be a mess.

My personal preference is to take screen shots of the demo and have them ready as back-up materials.

Involve the Audience

You will feel more comfortable presenting if you have built some form of rapport with the audience. Most presenters do this by involving the audience early on in the presentation. It might involve asking them some questions or showing them a funny video or telling a joke. Whatever you choose, make sure you know it won't fall flat. Nothing feels worse than having the introduction fall flat and feeling like you are starting the presentation from behind the starting line.

You don't have to be a comedian. In most cases, a good story seems to help. Just tell it in a casual conversational manner that has been practiced. A great approach here is to use your story to tell the reason why your audience should listen to your presentation. Let the story tell the reason.

Don't Prance Around

Presenters who move around all over the stage are distracting and generally look nervous or uncomfortable. While a high level of energy may be desirable in your presentation, sage advice is that it should be visible above the waistline, not below it.

If you feel the urge to move about, make sure you are moving for a reason. For example, you may need to go across the stage to listen and show real interest in a question or comment made by an audience member. Don't be afraid to move. Don't be a prisoner of the podium.

Don't Talk Too Fast

A common error with new presenters is to talk way too fast. It makes you sound nervous and it's often because you are. Spend time practicing delivering a talk that you already understand well. Pauses and inflections on words can make a world of difference to your delivery. Ask leading questions and give the audience time to think about them.

Don't Try to Memorize Your Whole Talk

I often see school children preparing for debates and they have written down every single word they are going to say. They end up stumbling over it and don't sound like they are really speaking their own words. They also lose connection with the audience. If they get off slightly, they have a most difficult time getting back into their prepared remarks and the audience can smell their frustration. Use notes (or perhaps slides) to keep you on track but have very little information on them. Deliver the presentation in your own words each time. Ideally, it should sound like you are telling a group of friends a story that you are really excited about.

Don't Clutter Your Slides

If you use slides, don't have too much material on each one. This is the same error as over-preparing what you are going to say. If you have more than four to six lines on a slide or if you need to use a font smaller than, say, 20 point, you need to reconsider what you have on the slide. You want the audience to listen to what you are saying, not to spend their entire time reading what you have on the slides. In addition, if you have a lot on the slides, you will end up reading the slide to them anyway.

Use a Microphone if Necessary

I see a number of presenters who steadfastly refuse to use any form of microphone because "they don't need one." It can be very hard to realize what the volume level elsewhere in the room really is like. If in doubt, use a microphone. Otherwise, ask the organizer and/or the audience whether or not you should. If they say yes or even sound doubtful, use one. Do this before the time you need to start.

Turn Off Pop-Ups

If you are using a computer, be sure to turn off pop-ups. This is a rule that I still fall foul of occasionally. You really don't want instant messenger messages, VOIP systems like Skype, or personal e-mails appearing on your screen while making presentations. It just isn't professional looking. At a session I did earlier this year, I was constantly getting a chuckle from the crowd that I didn't understand. My friend Sandi Hardmeier (an Internet Explorer MVP) was logging off and on to her computer. A pop-up message kept appearing telling people that "Flamethrower Queen" was logging on. Worse still, I have heard stories of attendees who are acquaintances of the presenter changing their own IM names and then logging off and on to see a cute message appear on the screen. Turn these things off.

Also remember to turn off your automatic screen saver before the meeting begins. Having your screen go black or seeing fish swimming across your screen is very distracting to your audience. This may make an appearance at the end of your presentation during questions and answers (why do I know that?).

Use Stories as Anchor Points

While you will mostly be concerned with technical content, I have found it very useful to have a few substantial but related war stories to add to my presentations. Stories can provide memory anchor points for attendees later. Plus, they help break up a technical presentation which otherwise always has the possibility of being boring (most technical topics offer pretty dry content).

Jokes Are Great – But Be Careful!

Jokes and funny videos can be very good additions to your presentations. If necessary, check for publication permissions on any videos you use in public forums. I cannot stress enough how very careful you need to be to avoid offending attendees. Jokes or videos can go very, very wrong if you are not careful. Not everyone is a standup comedian. If you aren't, don't try to be. Keep your jokes dry in nature and deliver them carefully. Self-deprecating humor can be amusing but watch that it doesn't step over into making you look like an absolute idiot or completely disorganized. I have seen this happen on too many occasions.

Have a Backup Plan

An earlier rule said to make sure your demos work. This is critical. However, given the wide array of things that can happen to each of us, have a backup plan. Imagine that your computer won't boot five minutes before your presentation. What exactly is your plan for recovering from that? If you had a copy of your slides on someone else's system or on a USB memory drive and they included screen shots from your key demos, you could probably get by. Don't allow a situation to occur where attendees go to all the effort to arrive, only to have the presentation be pointless or not happen.

Handling Questions and Answers

Be prepared to answer questions related to your session. Don't be frightened of these. Consider tricky questions as your chance to learn something from the presentation too. No one knows everything. When asked a tricky question, be confident enough to say, "I don't know." Everyone else in the room is probably thinking the same thing anyway.

Try to keep questions on topic. If someone starts to ask about things that are off topic but still in your area of expertise, suggest taking them offline. Don't use this as a cop out for things you don't know. Don't pretend to know an answer when you don't. Don't waffle or do the politician's trick of answering the question you want to answer rather than the one actually asked. Audiences can smell fear and BS a mile away.

If you have too many questions for the allocated time, tell the audience this and again offer to take them offline.

Accept Criticism and Learn

Attendees will often rate sessions poorly for reasons that have nothing to do with the session. My favorite was from a training centre that asked a student why they rated a particular class so low. His answer was that he didn't like lunch. You can't take things like this to heart. However, you should treat each and every presentation as an opportunity to learn.

My preference is to ask other experienced presenters in the room for candid criticism and for suggestions on how I can improve next time. I am fortunate to have friends who are very high quality presenters and I know they will tell me what they really thought of the session, good or bad. People who tell you, "Yep, it was good," and add nothing else to it are just being pleasant. There are always ways you could have improved the session. Find some trusted advisors and ask them. Be prepared to do the same for them.

Never Stop Learning

I think the day you stop learning should be the day you die. Every now and then, I get an offer to attend a variety of presentation skills courses. I try to attend every one of them. If you have a real interest in presenting, you should take every opportunity to have speaker trainers and fellow presenters critique what you are doing.

A good example of this is Microsoft TechEd in the United States. Companies such as Microsoft go to great lengths to make sure that all levels of speaker training are available to you before the event. At a recent TechEd in Boston, I had the opportunity to spend time with one of their "big room" speaker trainers. This was a great experience, but a little intimidating at the time. A complete, large seminar room was dedicated to this task. It was a room that could have seated four or five hundred attendees. The trainer started by meeting me and trying to put me at ease. He then got me to go up on the stage and start my presentation. The room lights were dimmed and the stage lights and spotlights were placed at the intensity levels you often experience in such sessions. The audio system was set up exactly as appropriate for a standard large room presentation. This means that you can barely see anyone in the room and you may as well be presenting to four hundred people as the two that were in the room.

About five minutes into the presentation, he made me stop and we discussed how I was doing. He was happy overall with my presentation but wasn't happy with the level of intensity I was putting out. He told me that on a scale of 1 to 10, with 10 being what he was after, I was about a 3. Most of the presentations I do are to rooms of ten to one hundred people. I tend to try to keep the session fairly conversational. I thought I was doing a pretty good job of it. So far, it had not really struck me what was needed for large rooms. The trainer pointed out that the Rolling Stones don't play coffee shops, and that people who play in coffee shops would need to do things differently if they played in a huge concert hall. He got me to increase my intensity significantly. After doing another session that almost completely wore me out, he told me not to ever worry about overdoing the intensity level. He said that I was still only about 6 or 7 on the scale.

The important thing is that the next day I did my session in a large room (and it was webcast as well), I did at least twice as well as I would have done had I not gone to that training session. I have done many hundreds of presentations over the years and yet I constantly feel the need to learn to do it better. What truly amazes me are the speakers who have offers of such training but don't take part. I can't begin to think why not. Courses that include video recording are especially valuable. Every presenter needs to spend time watching themselves present—if they wish to remove annoying habits or phrases or movements from their delivery.

The irony is that in many of the training sessions I attend, I've noticed that it's the better presenters who constantly come along and listen, not the ones most in need of help. Every time you have the opportunity to be trained, I encourage you to take advantage of it.

Summary

Creating and delivering presentations can be nerve-wracking for new presenters. Helping them get through this phase is critical for the ongoing success of your community.

In this chapter, we started by covering a number of tips for working with new presenters, such as advising them to limit the amount of material they prepare for their presentations, and stressing the importance of rehearsing.

We then covered tips and techniques used by experienced presenters: finding appropriate topics, structuring sessions, paying attention to timing and punctuality, and finding the right mix of demos and slides. We noted that screen fonts should be big enough to be seen from the back of the room. Make certain your demos will work, but have a backup plan in case they don't. Be sure to involve the audience through questions, safe jokes, or stories. Be aware of your movement on stage, and don't talk too fast. Don't try to memorize your whole talk and don't put too much material on your slides. Use a microphone if you suspect you need one, and don't distract your audience with screen pop-ups. When answering questions, you shouldn't be afraid of the tricky ones—these are opportunities to learn. Try to keep questions on-topic.

We also discussed the constant learning that all presenters should undertake. Solicit feedback, accept criticism, and take advantage of training opportunities.

FREE *Bonus:*

Greg Low's "Checklist for a Great Presentation" is available as a free download when you register this book at www.rationalpress.com. For instructions on how to register, see the last page of this book.

Part IV

Legal and Finance

Chapter 13

The Fine Print

This chapter discusses whether or not a formal legal association or corporation is necessary for your user community. First, let me stress that I am not a lawyer and that you should seek independent legal and financial advice that is relevant to your locale. These things really do differ greatly from place to place. What I provide here are things that you might wish to consider while making these decisions. We will also discuss the potential need for insurance coverage of various types.

Legal Requirements

A decision you may need to make early on in the life of your technical community will be whether or not some formal organizational structure is needed. This may mean something relatively simple, like the formation of a non-profit organization, but it might also require the creation of a more significant legal entity, such as a corporation.

Often, a decision on the structure will be forced by a decision on the funding of the group. Chapter 14 discusses funding options for your community, sponsors, annual fees, and meeting fees. In most countries, as soon as you have any sort of fees involved or as soon as you take money from any type of sponsor, you will need to have some form of organization in place. You might also consider some form of incorporation if it allows you to offset potential liability. We will discuss insurance in the next section.

For most of the user groups I have been involved in, we have steadfastly tried to avoid the need for a formal structure. I have seen many groups successfully operate on this basis, but I have also seen just as many work successfully within formal structures. My concern with formal structures is that they can tend to take on a life of their own, and the politics involved can easily overshadow the real community work that you want to do.

Even setting up some form of non-profit organization usually involves the creation of a set of by-laws, annual meetings, and elections. There may also be requirements on how the notifications of such meetings need to be made, and rules about how the meetings need to be structured and how the elections need to be held. Do not underestimate how messy this can all become. Your passion for community activities can easily be overwhelmed by committee meetings, minutes of meetings, formal meeting structures, concerns over positions, position titles, job descriptions, etc. Most people becoming involved in community activities have very little interest in anything reeking of bureaucracy.

Many technically astute persons are not good at the demanding nature of some formal structures (you know who you are). These individuals likely never dreamed of becoming not-for-profit gurus, so don't expect miracles to happen when they decline your invitation to take over some critical function within your formal structure.

Another hurdle you and your group management team will need to deal with when operating under a formal structure is the transitory nature of some members of your team. A formal structure may add to the long term stability of your group or it may cripple your group with a burdensome bureaucracy that your original members accepted, but your subsequent members may not be keen to join. Once you have an ongoing formal structure, you will need to maintain it or you may find yourself in more trouble with legal or government entities.

Over the years, I have seen countless people burned out by committees and political nonsense. These were good people with good intentions. Worse still, you risk losing them from the community completely.

Some years ago, I decided to help out one particular community. I was keen to devote a large amount of energy to helping them out. They were claiming to be a "global" organization, yet the entire board was from a single country. They were advertising for board members, so I decided to run for a position because I thought I could help broaden their perspective. On their Web site, they had listed details of the requirements for board members. I met all those criteria, so I applied. I thought it would then be a matter of the members of the organization voting for those of us who had applied. However, what occurred next was truly odd. Prior to the election, a group of existing board members culled the list of nominees to a much shorter list, according to criteria that had not been mentioned prior to that point. In the end, the existing board decided who the members were allowed to vote for. It reminded me of some sort of banana republic in action. In the end, the only nominees that the members could vote for were pretty much all from the same country. In speaking to other members, none were ever aware that someone else decided who they could vote for and that this sort of thing went on in the background. Consider the effect that this would have had on the nominees culled from the list. That would be the quickest way to take a group of dead-keen supporters and turn them into a group of disinterested onlookers. Do not burn out your best supporters with political nonsense.

Some of the technical communities I have been involved with were being organized by a group of volunteers, all of whom worked for the same company. If you have that situation, one option might be to get your company to provide the formal structure. They may be able to periodically oversee what you are doing but leave you free enough to get things done without significant interference.

Be careful when setting up a formal structure within a single company. In doing so, you may alienate competing companies, or just other companies that want to be associated with your group, but not necessarily affiliated even indirectly with your single company. If you set up a formal structure, you cannot delegate the responsibility to a company—that responsibility will become a deep part of your group.

If you are going to collect money, it is very likely that you will need some form of formal association or organization. In my country (Australia), I have found that meeting attendees will also want to be issued with what we call tax invoices. These can only be provided by organizations who are registered with the tax office and who file business activity statements on a regular basis. While the mechanics of doing this will differ from country to country, it is very likely that if you charge and receive cash or issue any form of receipts, you will need to set up some legal entity.

A number of the umbrella organizations can also help with this. For example, the Professional Association for SQL Server (PASS) provides specific assistance to their chapters (local groups) to help them with incorporation in certain countries. This could be a major benefit in avoiding complexities. In their case, they assist chapters in registering. All US-based chapters are registered in the state of Illinois. They also help with federal tax registration.

As another example, in the state I live in (Victoria), an organization known as Victoria .NET (www.victoriadotnet.com.au) has been set up to take on the legal role for interested parties in the state. A number of user groups from around the state have changed from being autonomous groups to becoming special interest groups under the umbrella of Victoria .NET. This avoids the need for them to incorporate and provides a legal basis and financial reporting structure. This allows the user group leaders to get on with the task of running their groups. It also provides insurance indemnity for the leaders in their user group-related activities.

As a final example, in New Zealand, a .NET organization (www.dot.net.nz) has been set up as a legal entity above all the .NET user groups in the entire country. It centralizes funding from sponsors and vendors and is also active in organizing activities that involve more than one member group, such as their SQL Code Camp (http://www.dot.net.nz/Default.aspx?tabid=94).

While we are discussing matters of a legal nature, you might also want to consider how you purchase Internet domain names and more importantly, who owns them. I have seen several situations where a community organization has wanted to part company with one of the original founders and move on in a different direction, but they struggled because that founder owned all the relevant domain names.

Similar issues can arise from who signs the checks and who has access to your funds or your legal status. There are many things to consider; this is just a taste of the many flavours of these formal structures.

Insurance

We live in increasingly litigious societies. Years ago, in my country, we used to watch television shows from the United States and see depictions of people being very quick to sue each other. We comfortably felt that it couldn't ever happen to us. That's no longer the case. This seems to be a global problem. I now see it happening in pretty much every country I visit. While it may seem unpleasant to have to consider the need for insurance, you do not wish to place your own family's future in any jeopardy through your involvement in a technical user community.

You may find that if you have a legal entity established on a non-profit basis, that office-bearers in that entity may be indemnified. You need to check this very carefully in your own country. Seek professional advice on this.

In general, insurance could be needed to cover a variety of potential liabilities. First, you may need some form of public liability insurance. This mostly relates to claims arising from people suffering some form of accident on the way to or from your meetings, or while they are in attendance. A simple example might be someone tripping over a power cord and breaking a leg. In many cases, the need for this form of insurance might be lessened if the venue you are holding the meetings in has arranged for this sort of coverage. Make sure you check.

Be careful if your venue requires some contract that you personally sign, because you may be liable. If you sign as a legal representative of your group, you may be taking on liability for the group. Again, seek professional advice.

Another potential liability is libel and slander. Laws will vary in different countries, but you might need to consider the following:

▶ What is your position if someone speaking at your user group makes comments that harm the professional standing of another member or even a non-member?

▶ What is your position if someone speaking at your user group unfairly criticizes a product or service in an unjust or untrue way?

▶ What if they release confidential material that they shouldn't have?

▶ What if you publish material on your Web site contributed by members and those materials are found to be libelous or slanderous?

▶ What is your position if material on your Web site contributed by members is found to be plagiarized?

▶ What if you organize an event, members incur substantial cost to organize travel to it and then you need to change or cancel the event?

▶ What if personal information about your group members is compromised either through negligence or on purpose?

I have no desire to curtail your interest in building a technical user community. In fact, quite the opposite. However, there are many situations in which some form of liability might potentially arise. If any of these concern you (and they probably should), you should seek advice on how best to protect yourself. If the personal risk is too high or the cost of insuring against that risk is too high, look into offsetting the risk via incorporation or by joining an overriding organization that has the means to deal with it.

In most countries, the decision as to whether you are liable when something goes wrong will be determined by whether or not you have a duty of care to the person injured. This can be interpreted very broadly in some countries. You owe it to your family or loved ones not to leave yourself exposed to any such risk.

Summary

This chapter discussed issues that might help you decide if a formal legal association or corporation is necessary for your community. Again, let me stress that I am not a lawyer and that you should seek independent legal and financial advice that is relevant to your locale. The advice will be different in different countries and may even differ greatly from state to state within a country.

A formal organizational structure may be something simple, like the formation of a non-profit organization, but it might also require the creation of a more significant legal entity, such as a corporation. Your method of funding may dictate which kind of structure you need. Remember that a formal structure may add to long term stability, but it might also burden your group with a bureaucracy that your members may grow to dislike.

We also discussed the potential need for insurance coverage and some areas in which liability might exist.

"How was I supposed to know we had to put choking hazard warnings on the name tags?"

Chapter 14

Funding

When user group leaders get together, one topic that often arises is how much to charge for user group meetings, events, or services—or whether to have any charges at all. In this chapter, we look at several of the issues that can help you make those decisions.

Free or Not Free. That is the Question.

Here at the very beginning of this chapter, I must state my bias. My strong preference is to avoid ever charging users for attending meetings of any user group I am involved with. I won't say that's the only way that works, but it is how I would prefer to see community events. I might feel slightly differently for special events that are out of the normal cycle of meetings, or those that require equipment or venue hire. Even there, try your best to keep yourself an arms-length from touching money.

By direct contrast, fellow MVP and friend Nick Randolph managed the Perth .NET Community of Practice for many years and his community charged an annual fee. The community success did not seem impacted by the need to charge a fee.

As mentioned in Chapter 13, one issue you will need to consider is whether or not you create a formal legal entity for your community. If you don't do so, you might not have whatever structure is required to accept cash and issue receipts in your country. In which case, you may be left with only two alternatives: don't charge, or set up a legal entity.

While a decision on whether to charge for user group meetings or services might not be a straightforward one, the following list of pros and cons might help you to decide that.

Positive Aspects of Charging Fees

Even though my preference is to avoid charging fees, there are some potentially positive outcomes of doing so.

Venue and Catering Costs

Rather than being dependent on the generosity of the owner of a venue or a sponsor, a pool of available cash places you in a much stronger position when making decisions about where to meet and about what level of catering to provide.

My preference has always been to find a key vendor or member who has meeting facilities available and is willing to donate them. If you do this, you need to be very respectful of that arrangement. Do not mess around with schedules. Plan your meeting schedule long in advance in conjunction with them and stick to it. Make it very clear to your members that they are guests at the venue. Always thank the venue owners at each and every meeting and make it clear to members how important it is to not leave any mess after the meeting. Ideally, the owner should not be able to even tell that a meeting occurred in the venue.

Speaker Travel Costs

While my main focus is always on growing speakers from within the community, having a high quality speaker from another area can be a wonderful change for the members. It can also help draw bigger crowds to the meeting, including potential new members you have not seen before. Moving speakers around can be costly. Having a pool of cash available to you can help you provide this for your members.

Alternative approaches to this can be tough to implement. With a little work and coordination, you might be able to find one or two local companies that would love to utilize some of that speaker's time while they are in town. They may be willing to share in the cost of bringing the speaker to town. You might also communicate with potential speakers and let them know that you'd love to see them if they are ever in town and to let them know your meeting schedule. Tell them that you'll try to be as flexible with scheduling their talks as possible. They may find a way to visit you without cost.

Some programs operated by vendors, consulting companies, and book publishers may offer their employees and authors as speakers and usually pay for all expenses for their people. Some individuals may pay their own way as a part of continuing their participation in vendor recognition programs (like the Microsoft Most Valuable Professional program).

I find I simply have a great desire to help out groups that I find really genuine. For example, in my inbox at present is an e-mail from a group from the other side of the country asking if there's any chance that I'll be in their part of the world and would consider coming to speak. What is most impressive is the invitation for my wife and me to both come and stay with the user group leader's family during our stay. I can tell this person genuinely wants to help his group and I know that I will go there if there's any way I can manage it. I also know that we'll be well looked after if we do.

Negative Aspects of Charging Fees

While we have seen that charging fees can have a number of positive outcomes, there are some pitfalls that need to be considered.

Elevated Expectations

Many years ago, I was lecturing at a university. During the time I was working there, the government introduced fees for the university courses. Students could opt to pay the fees up front or they could defer their payments through the country's tax system. The important thing was that even though the fees that the students were charged were a fraction of the total cost of providing the courses to them, their expectations changed overnight. Suddenly, there was a tone of "I'm paying for this" and greatly elevated expectations that simply weren't there beforehand.

You may find that as soon as you start charging any form of fee, your members' expectation levels for quality and consistency will rise significantly. Chris Wallace mentioned that he had seen the true dynamics of a group change over time when group members are paying dues of some sort. Sometimes this is manifest in the simple act of attending a meeting. Members may be called upon to sit at the door and grant entry only to those who pay, or keep track of people who come as a guest more than once. All this, in his opinion, is a waste of time and resources that could better be spent on creative ways to get people in the door rather than being gatekeepers.

Organizational Structure and Accounting Requirements

As mentioned earlier in the book, as soon as you have a requirement to collect cash, you are likely to need an organizational structure to support dealing with it. In particular, you will then usually have a set of accounting requirements to deal with. In some countries that might be as simple as a set of annual financial returns, but in other countries, it might require higher degrees of reporting and record-keeping.

Where this is required, it is likely that much more formal positions will need to be established within the organization as some person is likely to need to be elected or appointed to manage the finances. Another issue is that you might then be required to have an official street address for the community. For some communities, that can be awkward, because individual members might not be keen to have their personal addresses used for the community; it might need to change as office bearers change and the community may well have no actual street address of its own.

Most communities will require some form of delivery address anyway, unless they never intend to receive swag or samples from sponsors or vendors.

The Need to Make Commitments on Deliverables

If you decide to charge an annual fee, you may find that members will come to have specific expectations on what you will provide during the year. If you usually have twelve monthly meetings per year and you only end up being able to have ten of them, will they expect a refund of one sixth of the annual fees? You can avoid most of the problems by the careful wording of any agreement that the members accept when paying their annual fee. Regardless of the legalities involved, it is easy to have a situation where members feel short-changed. Be careful if you introduce a membership contract describing what members expect to get and how money is spent. These seemingly good documents can become the rope to hang you with.

Impact on Volunteers

You may also find that as soon as fees become associated with your community activities, it may become harder to attract volunteers. There is often a perception that "someone at some level is receiving cash that is being collected, so why should I be volunteering my time?"

Sponsors

While gaining some funding or prizes via sponsorship might seem to be an obvious desire for most communities, there are a number of issues in dealing with sponsors that need to be considered.

Sponsors Must Offer Value

This is my first golden rule when dealing with sponsors. Any community I organize is not an advertising agency or marketing arm for a sponsor. I endlessly receive e-mails from sponsors telling me, in fact urging me, to let members know about the latest thing that a vendor is so excited about. I place each and every one of these in the bin unless there is a genuine offer that will directly benefit members of the community. The first test I apply is that the vendor must be offering something that is not being offered to the general public—something that is only being offered to people who are members of our community. The second test is that it needs to be something that is likely to be of interest to members of the community and related to the aims of the community. While it could be argued that members of the community might be interested in an offer of a holiday in some exotic location, such an offer is unlikely to pass this test. The third test I apply is that the offer must be substantial. A five percent discount on a hundred dollar software product is not worth the time and effort involved in passing the offer on.

An alternative to placing these items into a circular file upon receipt is to offer the solicitor your local sponsorship program. State what your group will do for them and what you expect them to do for your group. Determine these guidelines ahead of time. Also determine what types of sponsorships your group is willing to accept. Will you accept only technical companies? If so, you are limiting your pool of sponsors. If not, are you willing to accept ads for your local car dealer or real estate company? You likely have a very desirable demographic and a captive audience each month, so make the most and the best of it, but always keep to your goals of being beneficial to your group.

Don't Sell the Farm (or Your Soul)

My second golden rule when dealing with sponsors is that I'd rather not deal with them if their offer comes with any significant ties. If we have to be seen to support a product that we really don't actually like, I'd rather pass up the sponsorship offer. Further, if the provision of sponsorship removes your community's independence or severely restricts its activities in any way, you should also pass up the offer. You still need to be in a position to always do the right thing by the members. The community is all about the members' interests, not about the interests of any vendor or sponsor. Never agree to sponsorship exclusivity. Keep your options open and shop around.

Don't Lose the Ability to Offer Critique

Another important aspect of your dealings with sponsors is that your relationship with the sponsor needs to be mature enough that the sponsor understands that you won't always be glowing in your praise of every one of their products. For example, if a product review from one of your members is critical of one of a sponsor's products, you don't want to be in a position to have to censor that material. At one event I was speaking at recently, another speaker had started to describe his successful experiences with a product. Within moments, the organizers of the event were signaling him to stop talking about it because the product was a direct competitor of one of the key sponsors of the entire event. You do not want to end up in this situation. Do not let a sponsor buy your silence on things they are not doing right or on what their competitors are doing well.

If you ever get to the point that you are making decisions about what would or wouldn't be appropriate topics for meetings on the basis of what a sponsor will think, you need to step back and take a long hard look at where you have allowed yourself to be led.

Summary

In this chapter, we looked at both the positive and negative aspects of charging fees for user group or community meetings or services. We also considered the impact that sponsorship might have on your group and techniques for minimizing undesirable impacts.

Part V

Extras

Index

CULMINIS
By the Community for the Community

Culminis is the independent voice of the IT Pro Community.

Representing over 500 member organizations in a 100 countries and over 3 million IT Professionals, and steadily growing, Culminis is the world's largest international not-for-profit independent organization powered by dedicated volunteers and is devoted to the development and growth of the IT community. Culminis provides services to support leaders and connect user groups, associations, and student IT organizations. Culminis stands committed to the free exchange of resources, ultimately elevating the status of the IT Professional both in their industry and in the community.

Join Culminis   www.culminis.com

Our mission is to support the development and growth of a strong and vibrant IT community. The technical and geographic diversity of our membership brings a wide range of knowledge and experience for the benefit of all.

Member Benefits

Listed below are a sample of the growing list of free benefits provided to our Member Organizations.

Community Development
Facilitate the continued growth of IT User Groups and Associations

Relationship Mapping
Provide IT User Group and Association leaders a point of contact with other leaders worldwide

Event Support
Promote and facilitate sponsorship of user group led events

Hosted SharePoint Site
Run your group or association using SharePoint

Participation
Recognize & reward volunteers, leaders and user groups

LiveMeeting
Free accounts for user group leaders

TechNet Subscription
Free account for use by user groups

Course Discounts
Up to 50% discounts on online commercial training courses

Public Speaking Aids
Special support and programs from ToastMasters

INETA: THE FACE OF .NET

INETA provides structured, peer-based organizational, educational, and promotional support to the growing worldwide community of Microsoft® developer user groups. Our mission is to offer assistance and resources to community groups that promote and educate their membership in Microsoft's software development technologies. INETA welcomes all facets of the Microsoft software development community, from developers and architects to project managers, graphic designers, and other software professionals.

By, and for, the User Group Community

Conceived and developed from the ground up by community user group leaders, INETA is committed to the software development community and to facilitating its growth and development. In taking on the responsibility of being an open and independent coordinator for user groups worldwide, INETA places a high priority on listening to the needs of its member groups and responding to them with tangible – and workable – initiatives.

Community driven user groups exist across North America and around the world. These groups represent an excellent opportunuty to learn and intereact with other professionals in your area.

To learn more about INETA groups in your area or help in starting one, please visit us on the web at

www.ineta.org

Join an Extraordinary

SQL Server Community

The Professional Association for SQL Server (PASS) is an independent, not-for-profit association, dedicated to supporting, educating, and empowering the Microsoft SQL Server community.

Connect
Local Chapters, Special Interest Groups, Online Community

Share
PASSPort Social Networking, Community Connection Event

Learn
PASS Summit Annual Conference, Technical Articles, Webcasts

Volunteer-run by SQL Server professionals for SQL Server professionals.

Join Today! Membership is Free.
www.sqlpass.org

Connect. Share. Learn.
w w w . s q l p a s s . o r g

USER GROUP SUPPORT SERVICES

MOVING FORWARD TOGETHER

SUPPORTING USER GROUPS WORLDWIDE IN
PARTNERSHIP WITH CULMINIS, INETA AND PASS

Get Your Group Moving!

As a Community Leader you know what you need:

- ◆ Extra money for your events
- ◆ People at your meetings
- ◆ Something to talk about!

We can get you there!

Get Extra $ for Your Events!

Microsoft, in partnership with Culminis, INETA and PASS now offers funding for your next community-led event! Whether it's a monthly user group meeting, a product launch event, or a code camp – whatever the format invite UGSS!

Get People at Your Events!

We know that in order for an event to be successful, you've got to have people there! **Add your events to our Global Events Calendar and gain publicity for your events worldwide.** This calendar is synced with other community calendars such as the Community Megaphone, and calendars on INETA and Culminis organizational websites.

Get Great Stuff to Show!

We know that you are busy. You work hard, you are a dedicated community leader. Who has time to create content for each event? Take advantage of our services for your next meeting and we can provide the content! Our content library is growing... check in monthly to see what's new!

If you need something specific, please let us know!

Get all this and much more!

- ● Global Speakers Bureau
- ● Global Sponsors Bureau
- ● Event Management
- ● Member Management
- ● Soon to come additional language support

Get STARTED on UGSS.CODEZONE.COM

Get Help!

Contact **ugss@microsoft.com** for technical support.

We'd like to say "Thank You" to our valued partners:

Event Funding is subject to availability and Event Funding Terms and Conditions.

Microsoft

IMPORTANT NOTICE
REGISTER YOUR BOOK

Bonus Materials

Your book refers to valuable material that complements your learning experience. In order to download these materials, you will need to register your book at http://www.rationalpress.com.

This bonus material is available after registration:

▶ Checklist for a Great Presentation

▶ Bonus Chapter: "Making Your Mark"

Registering your book

To register your book, follow these easy steps:

1. Go to http://www.rationalpress.com.

2. Create an account and login.

3. Click the **My Books** link.

4. Click the **Register New Book** button.

5. Enter the registration number found on the back of the book (Figure A).

6. Confirm registration and view your new book on the virtual bookshelf.

7. Click the spine of the desired book to view the available downloads and resources for the selected book.

Figure A: Back of your book.